MENOPAUSE
AND
MID-LIFE

ROBERT G. WELLS, M.D.
AND MARY C. WELLS
Director and counselor, The Menopause Center, Long Beach, Calif.

LIVING BOOKS®
Tyndale House Publishers, Inc.
Wheaton, Illinois

Notice: The information in this book is true and complete to the best of our knowledge. The book is intended only as a guide. It is not intended as a replacement for sound medical advice from your doctor. Only a doctor can include the variables of an individual's age and medical history needed for wise medical advice. Final decisions about any medical action must be made by the individual and her doctor. All recommendations herein are made without guarantees on the part of the author and the publisher. The author and the publisher disclaim all liability in connection with the use of this information.

Some of the material in chapters 3 and 4, originally written by Robert G. Wells, M.D., for publication in the January/February 1989 issue of Senior Patient *and the November 1, 1989, issue of* Postgraduate Medicine *(vol. 86, no. 6), is used by permission from McGraw-Hill, Inc.*

Living Books is a registered trademark of Tyndale House Publishers, Inc.

First Living Books edition October 1994

Library of Congress Catalog Card Number 90-70372
ISBN 0-8423-3975-2

Printed in the United States of America

02

12

ACKNOWLEDGMENTS

We wish to thank Diana Noller and her husband, Bill, acquisitions director for Tyndale House Publishers, for their inspiration and challenge to write a book about menopause.

Thanks to Sealy Yates, our friend, lawyer, and literary agent who, working together with Tyndale's senior vice president, Dr. Wendell Hawley, made it all happen.

To Tyndale's very talented acquisitions director, Ken Petersen, our sincere gratitude for his sensitivity to what we have wanted to communicate to our readers and for so skillfully bringing the material together.

And to each member of our staff who has worked with us in the Menopause Center goes our deep love and appreciation. These are the women who have worked tirelessly and faithfully with us, sharing our dream from the very inception of the center.

But the most important acknowledgment of all, we believe, is to the Lord. He gave us the strength to write and rewrite when we were bone tired. He enabled us not to lose sight of the goal he had placed in our hearts—to educate mid-life women, to encourage them to make wise choices that can lead to a better, more stimulating, and productive life.

Bob and Mary Wells

CONTENTS

PREFACE

My wife, Mary, and I have written this book to give women new hope and new direction for their mid-life years. In these chapters we will explain what menopause is, what symptoms it is responsible for, and how they can be treated. We will discuss the latest medical research regarding estrogen replacement and wade through the complex issues that accompany its benefits and risks. We will investigate common medical questions regarding menopause, osteoporosis, heart disease, and uterine and breast cancer. This book will offer you all the information you will need to decide, along with your doctor, whether estrogen is for you, and if it is not, for whatever reason, you will find one chapter devoted to the many options available to you.

We will talk about how menopause affects sexuality and how sexual desire and enjoyment can be heightened during these years. We will explore how a woman can maximize her health in her middle years. An additional chapter is targeted to husbands as to how they can be willing and effective in making their partners' transitional years more comfortable. Finally, in our Question and Answer chapter at the end, we will answer many of the questions about both menopause and mid-life that we, in our work with women at the Menopause Center of Long Beach, are frequently asked.

Our goal is to share with you our years of personal and medical experience. It is *not* a one-sided presentation, for we know that only when you have seen both sides of the issues will you be in a position to choose for yourself exactly how *you* would like to manage your menopause and mid-life, and then, and only then, can you remain totally comfortable with that decision.

Although we have in this book emphasized "husbands" and "wives," we are aware that many women are now single, unmarried, or widowed. To try to address every situation becomes lengthy and confusing. So if you are not married, please adapt and tailor the material we present to your own situation.

ONE

❧

Surviving Menopause: Mary's Story

STRANGE stirrings were creeping into my mind and body. I was aware that something was going to happen. There was nothing specific, nothing I could put my finger on. Not yet anyway. Just a feeling . . .

Bob and I were living alone in the big old ranch-style home where we had raised our three children. Now they were adults, happy and contented in their own lives. When our last child left home, I thought, *Now Bob and I can get reacquainted with each other. Maybe we'll even be able to put a little romance back into our lives and become closer than ever before.* Yet even with these opportunities for intimacy and "sexual appreciation," I felt myself withdrawing, first mentally and then physically. Only then did that vague and vexing feeling become clear enough to identify. I finally knew what it was. It was sexual—I had lost my desire for sex!

Lack of libido was among the first of many symptoms I was to experience as I entered the menopausal phase of my life. As I look back, I think I suffered almost every symptom of menopause while at the same time did battle with many different mid-life stresses. It was almost unbearable. Symptoms, anxieties, one after the other, washed into my daily routine. I would awaken in the morning and ask myself, *Well, Mary, what are you going to do today?* Better I should have asked, *What* can *you do today?* Not only was I immobilized to the point of being unable to deal with life's urgent needs, I didn't even care. I felt utterly bored with life.

When I faced the mirror in the morning, I saw a wrinkling face, graying hair, and a look of emptiness in my eyes. *The real me has got to be in there somewhere,* I would say to myself. I noticed, too, that every joint in my body ached. My feet hurt so badly I could barely walk. I felt like I had been in a bad accident, and everything I did seemed to take such great effort!

As depression set in, one day blended into the next. After nine, maybe ten, months I still couldn't muster up interest for anything or any-body. I had turned into a "middle-aged couch potato." Often I would ask God how long I would have to live in this void, live with this lack of interest in life, this feeling of hopelessness. I tried telling myself, *I'll get over this soon. Maybe I just need to do something new and different—to get my mind off of myself.*

But what? I wasn't even able to organize my thoughts, let alone where to store my grocer-ies! There were times when I would find toilet paper in the refrigerator or canned goods in the linen closet way at the other end of the house. I would cry over everything or nothing at all. I would even get choked up folding my hus-band's socks or watching leftovers grind up in the disposal. It was ridiculous! I had boxes of tissue in almost every room of the house.

I was sure my husband suspected something major was happening, something besides just me missing the kids. Then I sensed Bob with-drawing from me. Who could blame him? I was often critical and sarcastic with him. And that wasn't me. Besides, who likes being around a negative person? And I was the ultimate grump!

Obviously I was feeling sorry for myself and yet at the same time angry at not being able to accept the changes that were taking place in my life. Instead of enjoying my freedom with my husband, unencumbered by kids and their plans, I was wasting that precious time—doing nothing.

Often Bob would suggest we go to a movie or ask friends over for dinner or even eat out. More than not I would offer feeble excuses why we couldn't. It wasn't long before Bob had had more than he could take and blurted out, "What's wrong with you, anyway, Mary? Everything I try to do to cheer you up you say no to. You're so negative!"

I responded, "Why don't you ask me what *I* want to do for a change? How come we always have to do what you want to do?"

Bob retorted, "Well, what do you want to do?"

Then shouting at him from the top of my lungs, I said, "I don't know! I don't know what I want anymore!" As my anger and frustration were intensifying, I realized by the expression on Bob's face that I was fast losing control of myself. I was definitely not the calm, easygoing person he had married twenty-six years ago.

Now at this point, I know what you're thinking. If this is menopause, how could the woman's husband not have known what was going on if he was an obstetrician/gynecologist? Well, first of all, I went through menopause before Bob really came to appreciate the unique role of the emotions in the menopause syndrome and also before he became a specialist in menopause. Though he was a doctor, menopause then was a distant reality, and I, for one, knew nothing about it. From Bob's perspective I was still having periods, though somewhat irregular. I seemed healthy except for my complaints about my joints. The emotional changes I had just didn't seem that serious to his medical mind. Besides, his patient load at the office was impossible. Added to that, he had just lost his closest friend to a sudden heart attack, and he himself was reeling emotionally from that unexpected loss.

But when I told him about the heart palpitations and night sweats I was having every night, I hit a medical nerve. Bob told me it was time to see my doctor. Of course, my doctor happened to be my husband.

Two days later I was sitting in Bob's waiting room. For the first time in weeks I made a special effort to look sharp. I looked around the crowded room at my husband's patients. I thought to myself, *They probably think that I must really have my life all together. Wouldn't they be surprised to know that I'm the doctor's wife and falling apart physically and emotionally.*

5

The self-talk continued. *No, I'm not. I'm not losing it. I'm OK. It's just going to take a little time to pull myself together. Bob will know what to do.*

No, I'm not going to be OK. I'm a nut case and probably will end up in some psych ward somewhere.

Thoughts like this kept flashing back and forth, and I was getting more anxious by the minute. I could feel my pulse race. I wasn't worried about the exam, but rather about what Bob might find. How serious was it going to be?

Finally the nurse came out and called, "Mrs. Wells?" She brought me into the exam room and got me settled on the table and said, "Mrs. Wells, the doctor wants me to draw some blood and do an EKG."

The sample of blood would be used to run several tests, and among them an FSH (follicle stimulating hormone) to determine whether I was in menopause. The EKG (electrocardiogram) was to check out the heart palpitations. As I knew he would be, Bob was thorough.

Then the examination.

After I was dressed and was waiting in his consultation office for him I thought to myself, *What greater opportunity could I have to unload my fears and concerns.* I had made it a habit never to burden him with my insignificant problems at the end of his workday. For years I had handled calls from emotional women wanting to speak with my husband. Today *I* was the patient. I had my appointment. Now it was my turn!

A flood of emotions and tears welled up inside me. My doctor-husband said, "What do you think is going on, Mary?"

I replied, "I don't know, honey. But something's wrong. I feel so vulnerable, so shaky inside, and irritable. I've lost confidence in myself. It's as though every emotion or feeling I've ever felt in my life is surfacing all at once. I really am trying to help myself. I thought taking up golf would be good for us, so we could enjoy some activity together on our vacations. But now I hurt so much I can't even grip the golf club. Bob, I'm tired of all this. I'm too young to be old, and I'm too old to be young! I feel like I don't fit anywhere. I'm a mess. Life's no fun anymore. We're no fun anymore. And that's one thing that bothers me the most. I feel like you don't care about me, that you don't appreciate me. I know that's not true, but that's the way I feel!"

Bob let me unleash all my feelings and

frustrations. When I finished, he remained silent for a very long time. I could see he was thinking.

Then he said, "Sweetheart, I know you feel like you're—well, like you're a mess and a failure. But you're not. You're just not. I've asked the lab to do an FSH on you. You know, the test for menopause. It is very possible, you know. That could explain a lot of things that have been happening."

"Menopause!" I exclaimed. "Old people do menopause!" I broke into another round of tears. As I regained my composure, I said to him, "I suppose you've been listening to women cry all day."

"You're only the fifth one. It's been one of my better days," he said, smiling.

But I was in no mood for humor. "I'm going home," I said. "In fact, I might even change doctors!"

That night neither of us said much.

The next evening Bob sat me down and lovingly explained what was taking place in my body. "Your FSH, the test for menopause, is very conclusive. You're definitely menopausal. I'm sorry it took so long for me to recognize and diagnose it. I feel a little bit like an idiot—after all, I am a gynecologist!" He had even brought home some good brochures about menopause and estrogen replacement for me. I can't say I liked the thought of being in menopause too much at first. But the more I learned about menopause, the less upset I got about it. And I was certainly grateful to hear that there was an explanation for all my weird feelings and, better yet, something to treat it.

When I asked Bob what the risks of taking hormones were, he patiently explained them to me. He pointed out that going on estrogen, at least at this point in my life, seemed like a good idea. But the decision was mine to make. I knew I needed help, and hormones sounded a whole lot better than a psychiatrist's couch.

As we talked, I asked, "How long would I be taking them?"

He said that I might find myself wanting to take estrogen all of my life because of my family's history of heart disease and stroke. Estrogen, he explained, had been definitely shown to reduce a woman's risk of heart attack and at the same time protect her from osteoporosis. "The important thing is whether you should start now," he said. "I just want to see you happy and feeling better again."

As Bob talked to me about estrogen's long-term protection, it really did sound appealing because I'd seen what osteoporosis had done to one of my aunts. And the last thing I wanted was to live the golden years of my life as an invalid.

I decided to start on estrogen right away. In less than two weeks a sense of well-being had returned to my life. The crying had stopped, the night sweats had stopped, and at last I could sleep the whole night through. Best of all, I found I was able to concentrate more clearly. I was coming out of my nine months of depression. It was almost as if a cloud had lifted. And when this happened, I mentally recalled some loose ends in my life that badly needed attention.

Slowly, but surely, I realized how I had neglected our home during those long months of depression. I had not been able to focus on the things that made it a pretty and well-groomed home. But worse than that, we had pulled away from our friends. I didn't care what was going on in their lives. We had turned down too many of their invitations.

I knew then we needed some serious patchwork. We needed to open up our house again to friends that we had unwittingly pushed out of our lives. I knew it was all my doing! Entertaining had always been such fun for us! It was time to get going again.

It wasn't just relationships with friends that were breached but those with family, too. I knew I needed a lot of catching up with our children. When they would call me and ask for advice or favors, my excuse was always, "I don't feel up to it," or "We'll talk about it later."

That was not *me*. Usually I was always there for our kids and interested in what they were doing.

As wonderful as hormone replacement is, it wasn't a cure-all. But it did lift me out of the dumps and make it possible for me to regain some control of my life.

I was raised in a home where facing our problems, deciding what to do about them, and then having a positive attitude about them was our way to survive. So, how was I going to deal with my menopause, and how was I going to spend the rest of my life?

Menopause for me was the ideal opportunity to reassess where I had been and where I wanted to go. It was time to reestablish proper priorities.

I had felt confidence in the spiritual aspect of my life—my relationship with God, always so much a part of me—weaken. Could I, would I, be able to get that feeling back? That for me was a big question mark because I had felt spiritu-

11

ally dry, and that really scared me. I can remember one time sitting in church with Bob—tears rolling down my face. I felt numb, thinking to myself, *Is this what happens to people when they go crazy—when they disconnect from the world?* I felt no compassion, not even the slightest hint of interest for anyone else—not family, not friends.

I felt emotionally "used up." But I wanted and needed something new in my life, something that would change my attitude toward everyone around me.

Feeling a bit lonely one morning after Bob left for work, I found myself praying—something I hadn't done in a long time. "I need to talk to you, God. Do you still love me? Then give me new winds in my sail. Refresh me. Give me hope and meaning to the rest of my life here on earth. I resist change—you know that. But I also know you want to work in my life, to make me the kind of person you would like me to be.

"Father, there must be some women out there who feel as vulnerable as I do right now—women who are experiencing what I'm going through. I want to help them. Is that possible? Could I be an encouragement to them?"

After that we had many more "talks" together.

Bob and I spent the following weekend around the house. Bob was "on call." It was a beautiful summer day. A patient of his had given him an audio cassette about menopause. We listened to it together that Saturday afternoon as we sat in the backyard. As I listened I began to think to myself, *Someone should be doing something to help women like me get through menopause.* I knew I would never be able to forget how much I had suffered with it!

"Bob," I said when the tape ended, "why don't you make menopause your area of expertise? You've wanted to cut back on obstetrics, and most of your patients are older now and will be facing menopause soon."

As I looked him in the eye, I detected a spark of interest. My mind went wild, speculating, thinking how wonderful it would be for women like me to have a place where they could get help for menopause—a place where they could be educated as well as treated.

Bob and I spent the rest of the afternoon discussing the logistics of establishing a small menopause center. I became more and more enthusiastic. I could see my enthusiasm rubbing off on him as he began to pencil out what it would actually take to have a special center.

One day he came home and told me he had

presented the concept to his colleagues at work. They liked the idea so much they immediately approved it. "But I'll need your help, Mary. You haven't worked outside the home since I was in med school. What do you think about working a couple of days a week with menopausal women?"

"Yes, yes," I said. "I want to do this!"

Well, the prospects of a center really got my mind activated. I thought to myself, *Maybe this is how I can help others. I've been there. And who knows better about suffering and frustration than someone who's been there?* I knew this is what God really wanted for me—to help others get through this time of their life!

One day as I was combing my hair in front of the mirror, I stopped for a moment, stepped back, and took a good hard look at myself. I didn't *feel* old, thanks to estrogen, but I was definitely starting to look old. My hair, once a dark shiny brunette, was sprouting too many gray hairs. *When did this happen?* I thought to myself. *It's growing like crabgrass, and I didn't even notice.*

I leaned closer to the mirror and saw a million, yes, a million tiny wrinkles around my eyes plus a few sags I'd never noticed before. This was a time for total honesty. I was not looking at a well-groomed, pretty woman. My makeup was all wrong. My skin looked dull and splotchy, and where did all that peach fuzz come from?

I sat down on the bathroom stool and began to think, *How can I be of any use to others if I'm so drab-looking myself?* Sometimes buying something new or trying a new hairstyle does wonders for our morale. (I'm sure there are at least a few women reading this who will understand what I mean.) So off I went that very morning in search of a new image. *It can't hurt anything,* I assured myself. *Anything is better than what I've been through this past year.*

As I drove to the mall, I thought, *Lord, I want to have a new me on the outside. I want to look good again. I want to look young! But give me the courage to let you change me on the inside as well.*

After several trips to the cosmetic counter at my local department store, I learned how to apply my makeup in such a way as to enhance the good features of my face—to soften my "wisdom wrinkles," as I called them. Next came my hairstyle and color. I had been in a rut with the same style and graying hair for years. Believe me, I had earned every one of those gray hairs! Since I'd always wondered if blondes really did have more fun, I decided to go for it. I lightened my hair in stages. I didn't want to shock anybody.

Bob eventually got used to the color. He calls me his "blonde bombshell." Me? I love it. Blondes do have more fun. I told Bob, if my roots are showing when I die, please put the lid down on my casket. I'm gonna be blonde forever!

Next, I moved on to my wardrobe. It definitely needed upgrading. At the same department store I took advantage of their "personal shopper" at no additional cost to me. She helped me choose colors and styles that best complemented my complexion and figure. All this may not be your "cup of tea." Maybe your mate prefers you the way you are. I just knew *I* really needed this!

Regular exercise had never been part of my life, but I realized I needed to tone up my muscles. I also was aware of the need to cut back on the calories. I can tell you for a fact that I wasn't thrilled about doing either one—but something had to be done.

My favorite weakness in the whole world is butterscotch caramel sundaes. This is my idea of heaven on earth. The only problem is, when I eat it today, I wear it tomorrow.

It wasn't always that way. Once upon a time I could indulge myself around a buffet table three times without gaining an ounce. That was *before* menopause! Now the ounces were creeping into pounds as my metabolism shifted into low gear, and every sweet morsel I put to my lips ended up on my hips!

It had become increasingly difficult to keep my weight down as I inched my way up in years. It seemed as though I was taking on that matronly look. You know, the thickened waistline, the tummy bulge, the flabby thighs. Oh my!

I had to muster up some sort of discipline in my eating habits. So I *chose* to stop bringing goodies into the house for the kids when they came to visit us because I constantly set myself up for temptation. I also decided that when we invited people over for potluck dinners or desserts, I would insist the guests take the leftovers home with them. When we entertained, I donated leftover desserts to the nearest of kin or a neighbor. If that didn't work, I dumped it down the disposal before I ended up with telltale crumbs on my face and guilt in my heart.

I hate to exercise! My husband has named me the original "Unjock." Admittedly, I have never been successful as an athlete. I've never even come close. The only things I can do reasonably well are ride a horse and play golf. Nothing to shout about, but I do enjoy them.

I was invited to join a group of eight women in my neighborhood who walked on a daily basis. It involved taking a brisk, thirty-minute, two-mile walk every afternoon. No one likes to exercise alone, so I took advantage of the opportunity. When I first started walking, I was always a half block behind everyone else, and from time to time I found myself hanging onto a lamppost or tree, gasping for breath, or prostrate on someone's front lawn with some variety of pain in my anatomy. But after a while I became accustomed to their pace and began to feel exhilarated. We enjoyed talking and sharing so many topics of interest. It gave me a sense of accomplishment—and a dry mouth. I often wondered which moved faster, our mouths or our feet.

I'm glad to tell you that my story has a happy ending. I finally found the energy and motivation to go on to do new and challenging things with my life. I was determined to make menopause a positive experience. I know the estrogen helped pull me out of the depths. The make-over, new clothes, new diet, and exercise—all part of my personal program of self-improvement—helped me feel better about myself. But I truly believe that it was my talks with God that had the most to do with transforming my life.

But helping to run a menopause program brought with it another responsibility—one that I definitely need God's help with. And that is speaking at seminars or on TV or radio with Bob. Never in my life did I ever think I could do that, but it was the Lord who gave me the courage, even with shaking knees and pounding heart, to share with others my own experience with menopause that he allowed me to go through. God has made me a better person because I finally started to trust him for the results.

TWO

❧

Emotions, Self-Esteem, and Stress

EMOTIONAL symptoms are a common companion of menopause and mid-life. They are in part influenced by a woman's own perception of her changing body. Women are naturally and understandably sensitive to such radical changes taking place in their bodies.

But one of the greatest contributors to a mid-life woman's emotional swings is estrogen deficiency. The exact way in which lowered estrogen levels trigger these emotional changes in women is not clearly understood. It does appear to be initiated in the hypothalamus, the area of the brain intimately involved with our emotions. Brain cells in this glandular center are sensitive to changing blood levels of the two female sex hormones, estrogen and progesterone. Some women are more sensitive to these changes than others. This phenomenon may explain why some women have more difficulty with menopause than others.

EMOTIONS AND MENSTRUAL CYCLE

The best illustration of how estrogen influences the emotions is a woman's own menstrual cycle, where the ebb and flow of estrogen and progesterone cause distinct changes in her attitude and mood.

Let's walk with an "average" woman (realizing there is no such person!) through her twenty-eight-day cycle and see how her emotions tend to fluctuate throughout the month.

During the first week of the menstrual cycle, when the ovary produces estrogen in increasing amounts, a woman usually feels a surge of energy and ambition, and she's anxious to tackle new jobs or projects. She is assertive, positive, and wants to motivate those around her.

As the second week begins and the estrogen levels off, there is a gentle but noticeable transition—a mellowed, more relaxed, and mature attitude prevails. She is warm, loving, creative, sometimes whimsical, and she feels the need to take time to "smell the flowers." Lingering energy levels from the first week may even prompt her to plant some of those flowers! As ovulation takes place at the end of the second week, she still feels well. She is confident, compassionate, more passive, less assertive, desiring to be a lover and nurturer of her husband and family.

The third week is ushered in with the first-time appearance of progesterone. It comes on strong and forcefully. With it there is another slight increase in estrogen. These two hormones, rising in tandem, tend to evoke a restlessness in her. She feels less friendly, moody, discouraged. She's in the doldrums. She may have a foreboding sense that something bad is about to happen but cannot explain it. She may feel she is just "spinning her wheels," which adds to her confusion and frustration.

Week four, the premenstrual week, sees the estrogen and progesterone levels both falling. Tension and anxiety build. Little things irritate and annoy. She feels neglected, like no one is helping her around the home. She is torn between wanting to isolate herself—"Just leave me alone!"—and wanting to get closer to her family members. This mood change carried to the extreme is the "premenstrual syndrome" and is also associated with headaches, cravings, lack of energy, dramatic mood swings, irritability, anxiety, depression, and tears.

Finally, as her period begins, the tension leaves and her spirits lift. Once again she's rational and able to look optimistically at the world in a new light. She focuses on relationships and gazes at members of her family, thinking how wonderful, bright, and beautiful they are.

Of course, these are just tendencies. A woman is not a captive of her physical cycles. But a woman's physical nature week after week does have emotional effects, and sometimes they can seem quite mercurial. Author Jean Lush, who has written much about these changes, has said that "a woman's life is like sailing the ocean in a sailboat—calm and serene with gentle swells one day, then hurricane gales and tidal waves the next. Sometimes we wonder if we'll even survive!"[1]

MENOPAUSE—THE PROLONGED PREMENSTRUAL STATE

During the forty years of a woman's reproductive life, her personality is shaped to varying degrees by her monthly cycle. These cyclic hormone responses, especially the premenstrual ones, are likely to surface again in the menopause. One could think of menopause as a prolonged premenstrual state.

This should not surprise us as both menopause and the days just preceding menstruation have as their common denominator lowered estrogen levels. Depression, anxiety, mood swings, irritability, insomnia, memory loss, diminished self-esteem, and decreased interest in sex are just some of the symptoms with which many menopausal women struggle as a result of lowered estrogen.

MENOPAUSE AND EMOTIONS

The climacteric, the years that bracket a woman's final mentrual period, can be exasperating when a woman senses that something is wrong but feels helpless to change it. Candace, a soft-spoken woman of forty-eight years, had a look of determination on her face as she spoke to me one day at the Center. "Doctor, something is going on inside my head or body, something I don't understand. I've actually turned into a witch! I'm shocked at some of the things I say and do. I know when I'm out of control, but being aware of it doesn't make any difference. Things just spew out anyway! I'm hurting people I love. My kids tell me all I do is yell, yell,

yell! I'm critical all the time. I know I'm turning my husband off completely. It's as if every emotion I've ever had in my whole life is surfacing all at once. I know something is happening to me, but I'm powerless to do anything about it!

"I shared these feelings with one of my friends," she said. "She thinks it's menopause because she experienced these things herself. Do you think that's all it is—menopause?"

In her case it was.

Menopause and mid-life work in tandem. We might think of menopause as a woman's internal, physical upheaval and mid-life as her external, emotional upheaval. One seems to magnify the other, and it's difficult in most cases to root out which causes what. All we know is that in mid-life a woman experiences both internal and external events that can cause a variety of problems and a baffling array of emotional responses.

MENOPAUSE AND SELF-ESTEEM

During menopause, self-esteem is the most easily bruised part of the emotional anatomy.

One day Darlene sat across from me in my consultation office. "I feel so empty and worthless," she said. "No one needs me anymore. The kids and all their busy activities are gone. Now the house is so quiet! I miss my children.

John works all the time and doesn't seem to need me either. I feel as if my life is over. I have nothing to look forward to. I feel abandoned and useless. It's a feeling of insecurity I've never experienced before, and I'm just not coping with it."

Self-esteem can also be influenced by menopausal's memory loss and confusion. Evelyn was a vivacious, type-A personality, cosmetic sales representative. In one of her office visits she confided to me, "Last month I was driving on the freeway. My list of clients was on the passenger's seat next to me. After driving about five or six miles, suddenly and without any warning my mind went completely blank. I had no idea where I was or where I was going. I finally had to pull over to the shoulder of the highway and had what felt like a nervous breakdown. I cried and cried. It was devastating to realize I was not in control of myself. Since then I've noticed other episodes of confusion, and I have totally lost all confidence in myself. I find that I go back and double-check everything just to avoid embarrassing myself or letting people down. Dr. Wells, something terrible is happening to my mind. I'm afraid I'm getting Alzheimer's disease."

Later Evelyn was relieved to hear that lapses

of memory and mental confusion were symptoms of her menopause. We were able to treat her and relieve those symptoms, but until we did, they had worked a number on her feelings about herself.

MID-LIFE: A TIME OF STRESS

We must be cautious not to blame every physical ailment and emotional distress in mid-life on menopause. The is no question that estrogen plays a major role, but we are not products of hormones alone. Not only is the menopausal woman reacting to hormone changes in her body; she is also reacting to other events outside of her—especially those that cause stress.

Mid-life is a coming together of significant events (usually beginning around age forty) in a person's life . Some of these events are delightful and welcomed, such as grandchildren, more free time, and financial stability. However, for others mid-life can be a time when many rather stressful events occur at once—too many balls in the air to juggle. If we were to create a graph that measured the number of stressful events in a person's life from age zero to age one hundred, we would find that the graph would peak at mid-life, roughly the years between age forty and age sixty. Many of these stress events influence women more than men, partly because of a woman's instincts as a mother and caretaker, partly because in many families the man has defaulted on his responsibilities.

Teenagers

Women in their forties often have teenagers living at home, each struggling for his or her own independence. A mom knows that she should be patient with her "almost adult" child. But if that mid-life woman is also going through menopause, patience can be elusive. Her own mood swings clash with the even greater mood swings of her teen. It can become a stressful time of life and can contribute to the physical and emotional symptoms she feels.

The Empty Nest

The so-called empty nest is another mid-life stress with strong emotional consequences. It's one with which Mary can certainly identify. Actually, she was looking forward to our children's departure from the home. She thought it would be so much fun, just the two of us again like when we were first married. No more picking up after the kids, having to arrange our schedule around theirs, or worrying when they didn't come home on time.

We thought, *Hallelujah! Now we can have some peace and quiet!*

Wrong! For Mary, tears surfaced periodically as the time grew near for our youngest child to leave for college. He was our baby, and Mary was concerned about how he would manage twenty-five-hundred miles away from home. In our eyes, he still seemed so young.

When he did leave, the house became big and quiet. It doesn't take long for the mid-life mother (and father!) to feel the loss. Empty-nest mothers feel lonely and expendable, sometimes depressed. We both felt the loss of our children, but it affected Mary more deeply.

Unless a person has experienced the pain and loneliness of the empty nest, it is hard to understand the kind of stress that it brings. It feels a lot like homesickness, and it's not quickly or easily dealt with.

Boomerang Kids

Just when you thought it was safe to enjoy your life as a couple again, your adult child pops right back into your lives, needing help or a temporary home. The adult child may have financial problems, marriage difficulties, loss of a job—or, like Sarah's son, find himself in jail.

Sarah was one of our patients. "I have been

stretched so thin," she said, "I honestly believe there is no hope for a solution to my situation."

Her only son was in jail on an alleged murder charge. Sarah didn't have bail money. He called her daily, begging for help. Sarah's only daughter was hopelessly hooked on drugs and had run away. Sarah's husband wanted no part of what was going on, so he chose to leave home.

Sarah held her own for a few months until she developed a "shaky feeling all over inside." She was depressed, couldn't sleep, and finally went to a psychiatrist, but he didn't seem to help. As she put it, "He gave me three different kinds of pills to help me cope."

After a five-month period she was no better, and anxiety was getting the best of her. A friend suggested she come to the Center to see if there could be a physical reason for her problem. "It never dawned on me that some of these symptoms might be related to menopause," she said. The look on her face and the tone of her voice registered desperation.

Sarah is a perfect example of the stress that adult children can place upon a parent. And Sarah's case exemplifies how stress events can multiply in mid-life. Her son's problems led to her husband's departure.

Fortunately, we found that Sarah was in

menopause. While menopause wasn't the cause of her problems, it certainly complicated them, and treating Sarah's menopause with hormone replacement therapy helped her deal with the other problems in her life. Sarah met with our counselor, who helped her put her life back into perspective. It wasn't long before she stopped using tranquilizers. She struggled but eventually was able to put her life back in order.

Illness of a Spouse

One day Annie, a heavyset woman, sat down in my office. She looked frazzled. Her face was flushed. She let out a long sigh.

What I saw in her face told me she either had high blood pressure or she was suppressing anger. Twenty minutes into the interview I learned that Annie was feeling irritable. She was also unable to sleep at night.

Her forty-four-year-old husband was bedridden with an apparent terminal illness. She also had three young children to raise. When her husband died, she would have to find a job to support her family.

She had reached her limit. The hurt and frustration surfaced during our conversation. "I love him, but all I do is take care of him and the kids from morning till night. They don't care about me or what's going on in my life. You know what's going on in my life? Nothing. That's what!"

"There is something going on, Annie," I replied. "From all you've told me, it is possible you might be having some symptoms of menopause."

I reassured her we might be able to help her feel better physically, but she would be wise to see a counselor to learn to deal with her feelings toward her husband. She would need to make some practical decisions, too, such as learning about the care of the terminally ill from the local hospital's hospice program. She would have to consider a job later on. But in the meantime she would have to take it one day at a time. Annie felt encouraged about her situation once she realized at least part of her problem was menopause. Then, with some direction, she agreed to take action.

Divorce and Single Parenting

Unfortunately, another stress event common to mid-life is divorce. We have to remember that the real stress involved in divorce is the period before and after the actual legal event of divorce—the slow, painful dissolution of a relationship.

More often than not, divorce leaves a woman with custody of the children, and thrusts upon her the stressful role of single parent.

One day Mary had been interviewing a new patient at the Center. She stuck her head into my office and said, "I'm sure glad I had you by my side when we raised our kids!"

"What makes you say that?" I asked.

"Toni. You'll be seeing her next week. I just finished interviewing her, and I feel so bad for her. She's forty-one and has three teenagers—seventeen, fifteen, and thirteen. She just told me her husband left her four years ago for another woman—younger, of course. She spent the first two years just crying all the time, feeling abandoned, terrified of the future. Then the divorce became final."

Mary went on to tell me that Toni had become mother, father, and provider to her kids. But Toni was losing her confidence as a mom. She couldn't sleep at night, and she was irritable all the time.

Her ex-husband started another family of his own and was not the least bit interested in helping Toni or the kids. In addition, Toni was so afraid of failing in the role thrust upon her that she was physically and mentally exhausted. She worked forty hours a week and then spent the rest of her time managing her kids.

We didn't know how many of her symptoms were due to the stress of her suddenly becoming a single parent and how much was menopause—we never do—but it was a good bet that both were viciously at work at the same time. We ordered the test for menopause, which proved positive. Toni eventually went through treatment, including hormone therapy, and even though she still had to handle her stresses as a single parent, her situation improved.

Working Outside the Home

Stress in the workplace can be as great, if not greater, for women than it is for men. As there continues to be sex discrimination in the job market, discrepancies in pay between men and women for equivalent jobs, and lingering chauvinism in some business quarters, the mid-life career woman often finds herself having "to go the extra mile" to justify her raise, to achieve a promotion, or in some cases just to keep her job. When women do rise to top executive positions, some men accept it with reluctance and difficulty. It's not easy for a woman (for anyone) to get along with a coworker who resents her. The result is often chronic stress.

More often the woman who experiences this stress event is the single parent who is barely making it financially. What kind of stress is added to her life when a woman who depends on her work for a meager income suddenly sees her job in jeopardy?

So hats off, I say, to the working woman, whether she chooses to work or has to work. She works eight hours (or more), shops for food, cooks dinner, cleans what needs cleaning, and still finds time to be with her family.

Husband's Mid-Life Problems

Husbands are no less of a challenge to a wife's mid-life sanity because they too can find themselves in the crucible of mid-life trial. This places an additional burden on an already overtaxed wife.

Men, though they have no abrupt loss of their chief hormone (testosterone) as women do, can suffer as much psychologically and emotionally as women. Science one day may discover that a man's slow declining testosterone leads to his menopause—male menopause. But for now we can only call it "mid-life crisis." This is another subject and another book. But the point we wish to make here is that a husband's own mid-life crisis can become a significant stress upon a woman who herself is facing mid-life and menopause.

As we've already seen in the stories of Sarah and Toni, their mid-life problems were compounded by husbands who abandoned them in their time of greatest need. Each of their husbands probably experienced his own mid-life crisis, but the effect of his action deepened the stress experienced by his wife.

Aging

In mid-life a woman tends to look introspectively to see what she has or has not accomplished. She still has the same desires and dreams she had when she was younger, but now when she looks in the mirror, she sees signs of aging, not only in the face of the woman reflected there, but also in the rest of her body. She wonders whether she will have the vitality to pursue her dreams and ambitions. It's panic time.

She may become depressed and insecure. Her self-worth plummets. Doubt sets in as she wonders what she is going to do with the rest of her life. Life seems to be racing by so fast! Aging becomes a gradual horror and a significant influence upon her emotions.

Ruth, fifty-three, was a pastor's wife, married

for thirty years and completely devoted to her husband and his ministry. She described her husband as handsome, talented, and well liked in the community. She mentioned that she used to be active in the church herself but during the last few years had withdrawn from most activities. Ruth said she now felt wiped out and washed up, apathetic toward both her husband and her role as a pastor's wife. "I feel old, and I look old. Here," she said, "is a list of things that are wrong with me."

Mary scanned her list and noticed that most of her complaints aligned with menopausal symptoms. Ruth admitted she was depressed. Mary reassured her that if the blood tests confirmed that she was menopausal, Ruth would more than likely notice a difference with estrogen.

"How?" she asked.

Mary explained that after a short time she would probably begin to regain her confidence and have a sense of well-being.

"That will be a welcome change," Ruth said immediately. "I'm sure not the helpmate to my husband that I used to be."

Mary observed privately that Ruth looked drab and matronly. Mary didn't want to mislead Ruth into thinking that estrogen would take away all visible evidence of aging (it never does), so she asked how Ruth envisioned herself as a wife.

"I wish I looked young, vibrant, and energetic!" Ruth replied. "Right now with my gray hair and all, I look more like my mother-in-law."

"Do you really want to change your appearance?" Mary asked.

"I've just never quite had the nerve to do it."

During the next half hour Mary encouraged Ruth to improve her self-image by doing some simple things. It wouldn't cost a fortune for Ruth to upgrade her wardrobe a little at a time. Mary put her in touch with a personal shopper who would work within Ruth's budget at a well-known department store. That way Ruth could learn what colors and styles looked best on her. Next came her hair. She needed a good color to enhance her complexion and a style she could manage herself. And last came the makeup. For this she could get advice from the store's cosmetic department. They would help her learn how to apply her makeup properly to soften the lines in her face and make her look younger.

Realizing she needed to lose a little weight, Ruth joined an aerobics class at her neighborhood health spa. She took brisk walks twice a week with her husband.

When she came back for her second visit with us, we barely recognized her.

"Ruth?"

"Yes," she said, giggling. "It's me. I never knew I could look so pretty. My husband has found a new woman—and she's me!"

Ruth's earlier perception of herself as an aging woman who had lost her beauty was, as it is for many women, a self-fulfilling prophecy. She became depressed by the effects of mid-life upon her appearance and body. The solution was relatively uncomplicated. It simply required Ruth to take charge of her life—her appearance, wardrobe, and commitment to some exercise. Not only did it improve the way she felt about herself, it was a great opportunity for Ruth and her husband to make plans to live a more active life together. It revitalized their relationship.

Parenting Our Parents

Most every mid-life woman will eventually have to care for an aging parent. Our parents will one day depend on us to help them in areas of their lives where they are unable. And they deserve our help and attention, whether emotional, financial, or whatever. After all, in most cases they invested a whole lot of time in us. But their needs always seem to come at the wrong time. For example, it may hit when you are still trying to raise your children. Who has priority? It doesn't take much to feel "sandwiched," and even a little resentful, especially when they need you just when you are beginning to have a little time for yourself.

Elizabeth, sixty-three, drives more than two hundred miles every other weekend to visit her eighty-nine-year-old mother in a nursing home.

This devoted lady was full of resentment when she unloaded her burdens in my office. She told me she felt sore all over: "Every joint in my body aches, but I've just been told by my doctor I don't have arthritis.

"I'm worn out between visits to my mother, her daily phone calls, and lists of things she wants me to bring every time I come. If I don't, she has little ways of making me feel guilty."

I asked if her mother had other family members who could help.

Elizabeth replied, "Yes, but I'm her only daughter; she depends on me."

So often it is the woman—as daughter or daughter-in-law—who shoulders the care of invalid parents. This stress event has an enormous impact on the emotions of the mid-life woman. Combined with menopause, it can create significant strains on a woman's sense of well-being.

Death

It follows then that the mid-life years may be a woman's first contact with the terrible sting of terminal illness or death.

Some time ago Mary and I experienced the unexpected death of our closest friend. It was sudden—a heart attack—and his loss impacted every aspect of our lives. Ron had a charming, witty personality that entertained us all. He and his wife, Sharon, vacationed with us a lot. During those fun-filled years we became especially close—sharing our deepest feelings, praying for each other, and supporting one another— especially during the problem times in our lives.

Just six months after Ron died, Sharon discovered a breast lump. It had already spread to her lymph nodes. Radiation, chemotherapy, and an unyielding will to live were not enough to stop the ravages of Sharon's cancer. She died quietly in her sleep early one morning four years after Ron's death. Mary still misses her best friend, often feeling the urge to pick up the phone to call her, only to be painfully reminded once again of her death.

We all will experience the death of a loved one in our lives. It is in mid-life that the death of a friend or family member is most likely to occur. Death becomes part of the emotional fabric of mid-life and, for a woman, menopause.

The Fast Lane

One significant but often overlooked mid-life stress is the schedule we keep—otherwise known as the fast lane. Many people in mid-life find themselves in daily schedules that are just simply too busy and out of control. This may again be particularly true of women, who must keep pace not only with their own schedules but also with those of their children.

The mid-life woman finds herself still transporting kids before they can drive, coordinating school activities, and often planning family social and recreational activities. The older mid-lifer, often to avoid the empty-nest syndrome, may fill her life with social, community, and church activities that quickly swallow her up as those around her begin to depend on her more and more—especially if she has done a good job on some project.

In many ways I encourage women in mid-life to keep busy. Too many quit the race entirely and watch the rest of their lives from the sidelines. There's a part of us that needs to be needed, and activities with other people satisfy those needs and help keep us young and vital. But at the same time, schedules need to be managed. A mid-life woman needs time to rest. She should use mid-life as a time to enjoy the world around her.

The Persistent Stress of Childhood Trauma

One out of every four women has had a past history of sexual abuse—incest, rape, or molestation. Many women have suppressed it for years. The implications of this are shocking, and I wonder what price our society will pay (or is paying) for these tragedies.

We have noticed in our practice that these memories not infrequently resurface during the mid-life menopausal years. Why, we are not sure, but too often we see our patients relive the events in their consciousness or perhaps wrestle once again with their feelings toward the one who inflicted the abuse. Counseling for this mid-life stress is critical.

Obviously, stress is here to stay. It has become a part of this country's way of life. National surveys indicate that the negative impact of stress on performance—at work and at home—is not a media concoction. We have found in our work that nine out of every ten women who come to us for treatment of menopause are suffering from some type of ongoing stress in their lives that began even before they reached menopause. Fewer than half of them have taken any positive steps to resolve those sources of stress. Most seem resigned to the fact that stress will always be a part of their lives.

Many women bring already existing stresses with them into mid-life only to find a whole new set of stresses unique to the middle years. The compounding effect of the two, plus having to cope with menopause, can be oppressive and have significant effects upon women emotionally.

Regardless of whether the mid-life woman's emotional symptoms or self-esteem problems are the result of estrogen insufficiency or ongoing tensions of mid-life, they are real. They are painful. They are discouraging. They are *not* imaginary.

But a woman need not despair. There are solutions, and they all start with a healthy understanding of what menopause is.

THREE

❧

Understanding Menopause

MOST women face menopause with at least some degree of apprehension, a concern perhaps fanned by childhood memories when Mom's whole personality seemed to change overnight. As memory has it, she was suddenly on edge, irritable, crying for no reason at all. And Dad, sensing the confusion, offered a simple answer: "Your mother is just going through the change. We've got to be patient with her for a while. But she'll be OK. I promise."

But that explanation never seemed quite enough to explain the strange metamorphosis that took place in a previously calm and loving person. No wonder women in the middle years of their lives find themselves asking the question, *Is this what my children are going to remember about me?*

Actually, many women adapt smoothly to menopause. They may wonder, *Why all the fuss?* But for others it can be a nightmare, a time of testing that can carry a woman to the edge of despair.

A woman should not let menopause spoil her mid-life. And the best way to prevent it from doing so is to understand it and to take advantage of what medical science has to offer.

WHAT MENOPAUSE IS

The word *menopause* comes from two Greek words meaning "cease" and "month." It refers to a woman's last menstrual period—age fifty-one for the average American. Though a woman's final menstruation is a milestone in her life, she does not struggle with that. In fact, most women welcome it! But she does struggle during the years before and after that biological marker.

Those years that bracket a woman's last and final menstrual period are called the *perimenopause*. According to the American College of Obstetricians and Gynecologists' definition, this is "an interval of time . . . that precedes and follows that last period and is

characterized by waning ovarian function."
Some in the medical profession still refer to it
as the *climacteric*, but this is a term rarely
used by the public.

Whether we call it menopause or perimenopause, we are talking about a span of
years, perhaps ten to fifteen, that begins for
most women around their mid-forties and represents a time in which a woman often experiences menstrual irregularity along with
distressing physical and emotional symptoms.

The years that precede the last menstrual
period are known as *premenopause,* though
some are beginning to call it the *perimenopause*.
The years that follow, *postmenopause.*

It is important to point out that menopause,
unless brought on surgically, is a *natural* physiologic state in a woman's life in which the
ovaries age to the point that they cannot keep
up with the body's needs. Therefore, *menopause is not a disease!* It is simply the loss of a
woman's chief sex hormone—estrogen.

TYPES OF MENOPAUSE

Surgical Menopause
If the ovaries are surgically removed, most
often at the time of hysterectomy, ovarian

function stops abruptly. The production of estrogen, progesterone, and testosterone (the fact that the ovaries produce testosterone is a surprise to most women) comes to an immediate halt. It would be rare today for a gynecologist to remove the ovaries in a young woman and not replace at least her estrogen. But it has happened in the past with serious consequences such as osteoporosis and premature cardiovascular disease.

Natural Menopause

Every woman begins her life with approximately 2 million eggs (ova) in her ovaries. She draws from this endowment during her reproductive years of ovulation (the monthly release of the egg).

Each egg is nestled in a spherical cluster of cells called the egg follicle. It is from these cells that estrogen and progesterone, the two female sex hormones, are secreted during the reproductive cycle.

The huge number of egg follicles that a woman is born with are almost entirely used up during her forty-odd years of reproductive life. This is because each month many follicles prepare for the process of ovulation, but only one is actually chosen to release its tiny egg into the fallopian tube (occasionally two or three in the case of twins or triplets). The unchosen follicles are simply lost to the process of degeneration.

A delicate balance is present between the hormones produced in the brain and the ovaries. Follicle-stimulating hormone (FSH) and luteinizing hormone (LH) are manufactured by the pituitary gland, which is located at the base of the brain and under control of the hypothalamus, a gland that sits anatomically on top of it. The pituitary, urged by the hypothalamus, releases these hormones (FSH and LH) into the bloodstream. These hormones are really just tiny messengers that find their way to the ovaries and signal them to make more estrogen and progesterone.

Estrogen is the principal feminizing hormone and responds to the prompting of FSH. It is produced throughout a woman's monthly cycle. Progesterone, on the other hand, answers to LH and is produced only in the second half of the cycle after ovulation has taken place. Progesterone is responsible for preparing the lining of the uterus (endometrium) for pregnancy. If pregnancy fails to take place, both estrogen and progesterone production stop. As the concentrations of these two hormones fall, the endometrium is shed from the uterine wall along with some blood. This is the menstrual period.

The menstrual cycle functions smoothly through the cooperative effort of both brain and ovaries. Medically this is called the "feedback mechanism." When the hypothalamic-pituitary centers of the brain are satisfied that the body is receiving adequate amounts of estrogen, they shut off the production and release of FSH. When estrogen is elevated, the FSH level stays low. When estrogen is low, the blood FSH level rises, sometimes rather quickly.

DIAGNOSING MENOPAUSE

A doctor takes advantage of this reciprocal relationship between FSH and estrogen in diagnosing menopause. As a woman ages, so do her ovaries. Over the years the hormone-producing egg follicles are nearly all used up. Ultimately there are too few follicles to meet the body's demands for estrogen. The hypothalamic-pituitary centers, as if trying to flog the faltering ovaries, release more and more FSH. The follicle-stimulating hormone backs up in the bloodstream and will be found to be elevated when tested, affirming the diagnosis of menopause. It is an indirect method of getting at the truth about the current status of the ovaries. It is much more reliable than testing the actual blood levels of estrogen, which fluctuate too much. The actual FSH blood value that signifies menopause now varies depending on which type of laboratory equipment is being used. Historically anything greater than 30 miu/mL has been considered menopausal. Now the actual value will vary from lab to lab.

The ovaries are unique from all other glands (e.g., thyroid, adrenal, pituitary) in that they age prematurely and stop functioning before the end of one's life. The other glands continue unabated to manufacture their hormones up to the point of death.

So natural menopause starts with the loss of the ovary's hormone-producing egg follicles. Estrogen levels gradually decline. Ovulation stops. Progesterone becomes history. Though estrogen continues to be produced both by the ovaries and in peripheral fat tissue, it does so in lesser amounts until finally there is not even enough to stimulate the lining of the uterus, and periods cease.

That is menopause. But before that final period the lowering estrogen can have a profound effect on a premenopausal woman, both physically and emotionally. She can perceive this as a radical, traumatic change going on inside her.

WHAT MENOPAUSE ISN'T

Menopause is not a psychiatric disease. We are all thankful that menopause has been rescued from the Freudian chapters of medical textbooks and has been reassigned to a non-psychological classification where it belongs. It is out of the closet, and today there is an openness about the climacteric. The media is helping to educate women with the truth about menopause. Magazines are presenting more and more articles about menopause. Talk shows and news broadcasters are featuring open discussions about menopause and hormones.

So there is hope for the woman facing menopause. Gone are the days when women were left to their own devices to "gut it out." No longer are they pushed to alcohol, tranquilizers, or psychiatrists for solace.

Today we know that natural menopause is a perfectly normal endocrine disturbance—a deficiency of estrogen. Let us stress that this chemical imbalance manifests itself both *emo-*

tionally and *physically*. Because it is an endocrine problem, it can be treated through hormone replacement therapy.

THE SYMPTOMS OF MENOPAUSE

There are both long-term and short-term effects of menopause directly resulting from the lowering of estrogen in a woman's body. The long-term effects are cardiovascular disease and osteoporosis, which we will explore in chapters 5 and 6.

The short-term effects of menopause include the following:

Menstrual Irregularity

In her early to mid-forties a woman's levels of FSH will begin to rise slowly in response to declining estrogen. It is thought that the higher concentrations of FSH tend to ripen or mature the egg follicles more rapidly. Instead of taking the usual fourteen days, they may accomplish this in ten to twelve days. That alone can shorten the cycle by a couple of days.

Next, aging of the egg follicles causes them to lose their ability to mature to a point of ovulation. Failure to ovulate shortens the cycle even more. So it is not unusual for a woman in her forties to see the length of her cycles reduced to twenty-three to twenty-four days.

As ovulation stops, the protective hormone progesterone is lost. Its job is to guard the endometrial lining of the uterus from being overstimulated by estrogen. It accomplishes this by assuring a uniform and complete sloughing of the lining once a month (menstruation)—a kind of monthly "housecleaning."

Without progesterone, the endometrial lining of the uterus can become overstimulated by estrogen, leaving it thick, patchy, and uneven. At the time of the next period, it sheds haphazardly, causing the period to sometimes spurt and sputter.

In some women, persistent low levels of estrogen are unable to maintain the integrity of the lining during the middle of the cycle, and midcycle bleeding may develop.

The result of aging egg follicles is shorter cycles, a "different" kind of period, and occasional midcycle spotting. How and to what extent this menstrual irregularity occurs will vary from woman to woman.

Hot Flashes and Night Sweats
No one fully understands the anatomy of the hot flash, but medical science has uncovered

many interesting facts about this hallmark symptom of menopause.[1]

Virtually every woman who goes through menopause untreated will experience hot flashes. Eighty percent will have these terribly annoying symptoms for more than a year and 25 percent for more than five years. In 50 percent of women who experience hot flashes, these symptoms begin as much as five years before menopause while she is still having periods. Hot flashes can occur anytime but are usually more intense at night and are usually accompanied by profuse sweating, headache, and rapid heartbeat.

The classic hot flash is known medically as *vasomotor instability,* a reference to the rapidly changing diameter of the blood vessels of the skin. It begins for most women with a vague feeling or premonition that something is about to happen. And it does. Less than a minute later a sudden warmth is felt over the face, neck, and chest. This wave of heat usually lasts several minutes and is followed by a distinct redness of the skin for another five minutes or so.

"Those horrible night sweats" is the way women describe them when they are nocturnal. "Humiliating and embarrassing" is the way they describe the lobster-red flush and drenching perspiration that takes place in front of others during the daytime.

The term *hot flash* refers to both the aura and the sudden feeling of warmth—a subjective event. The "flush," on the other hand, is an objective change of skin color that can be seen by others, too—like a bad sunburn often accompanied by drenching perspiration. The flash is the feeling, while the flush is the visible change. Experiencing this in public embarrasses most women, which intensifies the flush.

One evening Mary and I were dining out with a group of friends. Shortly after we sat down and passed around the menus, Mary had a full-blown hot flush. As the others scanned the menu, Mary furiously fanned herself. She was still fanning as the waiter approached and asked for her order. "Order?" she said, "I haven't even seen the menu. I've just been using it!" We laughed, but we knew she was embarrassed. This is a common episode in the life of the menopausal woman.

The entire hot flash episode begins in the hypothalamus, the area of the brain located just above the pituitary gland. The hypothalamus has many functions. First, it is a glandular control center and is responsible for the regulation (via the pituitary gland) of such endocrine organs as the ovaries, adrenals, and thyroid. Second, it houses the body's temperature control center, charged with the responsibility of maintaining an ideal body temperature. Third, it plays a major role in our emotions. In fact, there are few, if any, emotional reactions that take place in our body that this tiny center doesn't know about or attempt to regulate.

The hypothalamus functions most smoothly in an atmosphere of ample estrogen. If the estrogen level is low, as in the case of menopause, and the hypothalamus is helpless to change it, the hypothalamus begins to act erratically.

The theory about hot flashes postulates that a hypothalamic "storm" erupts, accompanied by the release of adrenalinelike hormones that spill over into the nearby temperature control center, jarring it and causing it to inappropriately reset the body's core temperature downward—much like turning down the thermostat in our home. When this happens, a woman's body responds by doing everything it can to drop the core temperature down to this new setting. It accomplishes this by dilating the skin vessels (red flush), relying on conduction and evaporation (perspiration) to release heat out of the body to the cooler outside environment.

Sleep Disturbances

Medical science has shown that low estrogen levels interfere with sleep. Insomnia is in fact an early sign of menopause. Continued sleep disruption can significantly decrease a woman's energy level, sense of well-being, and ability to handle the stresses of daily living.

Some research investigators still believe that insomnia is the cause of all the emotional and psychological symptoms of menopause. These symptoms include mood swings, anxiety, depression, irritability, memory loss, confusion, and decreased interest in sex—the things many climacteric women experience. While I don't believe in laying every ill at the feet of insomnia, I can believe that continued lack of sleep is responsible for irritability, something to which everyone who has tossed and turned all night can attest.

Fatigue

One of the most common symptoms that menopausal women complain of is fatigue. Most victims of energy loss recite the same story: "I'm tired all the time. I just don't have enough energy to do the things I need to do. My doctors have done all the tests and have found nothing."

Emotional Symptoms

One of menopause's earliest signs, and often preceding hot flashes, is varying degrees of emotional changes, "mental pause" as some women jokingly refer to it. They can include depression, anxiety, irritability, crying for no reason, mood swings, memory loss, and mental confusion. I remember one patient, a secretary, telling me, "It was like the computer was down!" These symptoms are often more of a concern to the mid-life woman than the physical ones. They are particularly distressing because she knows they are happening to her, but she feels helpless to do anything about them.

Joint Pain

Another symptom many women have in menopause is multiple joint pain. Like fatigue, this too can be an enigma, for test results are also normal. Many of these sufferers have already been to the offices of internists, orthopedists, and rheumatologists who have found nothing. They often conclude it is probably the beginning of arthritis and prescribe aspirin in high dosages or one of the anti-inflammatory drugs. Neither helps much.

Vaginal Dryness and Urinary Tract Problems

Generally, vaginal dryness and urinary tract disorders make their appearance a little later than menstrual irregularity, hot flashes, insomnia, fatigue, and emotional changes. However, unlike hot flashes, which eventually disappear even without treatment, vaginal and bladder changes become progressively worse with time. Vaginal dryness occurs when the lining of the vaginal wall becomes thin and less distensible. This is the direct result of inadequate estrogen. Known as "atrophic vaginitis," it occurs at other times in a woman's life when estrogen levels are low, such as immediately after having a baby, during the months of breast-feeding, or often right after a period. Vaginal dryness can be one of the most disturbing menopausal symptoms a woman can experience because it causes painful intercourse that complicates the rest of the marriage relationship.

One of my patients confided to me just before her examination, "Dr. Wells, our marriage is in trouble, and it's probably all my fault. I've lost all interest in sex. I never used to be this way, but it's gotten so painful for me. Larry has been so patient, but lately I sense we're getting on each other's nerves. I know it all stems from my unwillingness to have sex. I just don't know what to do about it!"

Her pelvic examination immediately revealed the root of the problem—severe atrophic vaginitis. No wonder she had lost interest in sex. I could see how any attempt at intercourse would have left her hurting for days after. This patient didn't need counseling or reading or anything else. All she needed was a little reassurance and some vaginal estrogen cream. Within six weeks' time, with the return of her natural vaginal lubrication, a healthy sexual relationship was restored.

Jane, a new patient, came to see me at the Menopause Center one day. She said that although she had a good marriage of twenty-plus years, there was one area in which she felt she was failing. Over the past year she had had few sexual relations with her husband. She even told me some of the devious things she said and did to avoid sex. She also admitted that it was about to break up her marriage. "It's all my fault, Doctor, I'm guilty. I want desperately to save this marriage. I know my husband feels rejected, and

I also know he's beginning to notice other women more. I've got to get some help!"

Unless there is open communication, a shunned husband may feel frustrated, sulk, or get angry. A sexual barrier can even destroy a marriage. Sexual intimacy is important during the middle years when so many stresses exist. This is the time for couples to draw physically, emotionally, and spiritually close together, working as a team. Having a best friend in times of need is half the battle.

Simply using lubricants can help some, but many women feel sexually inadequate if they are unable to lubricate naturally. A husband might interpret her need for a lubricant as a deficiency on his part to arouse her sexually. Discouragement can even lead to his impotency, understandable since *the number one sex organ is still the mind!*

If untreated, vaginal changes continue to get worse. The vagina of postmenopausal women after years of estrogen deprivation becomes smaller, shorter, less elastic, and more vulnerable to injury and infection. Sometimes it can shrivel in size to a point where intercourse is virtually impossible.

The vaginal lips (labia) and clitoris are also estrogen dependent, and without this hormone, over a period of years, they will become smaller, more pale, and flat. This shrinking of the vagina and external genitalia is called atrophy and can cause a woman to feel sore and itchy all the time, not just with intercourse.

Bladder Problems

The nearby bladder and urethra also need and rely upon estrogen. Without it they too can become thinner and drier. Without estrogen, women may notice burning and irritation with urination or experience frequent bladder infections.

The postmenopausal woman may often begin to lose urine with coughing, sneezing, or vigorous activity (stress incontinence). This happens because the tissues of the pelvic floor, as the result of both estrogen deficiency and aging, can lose their tone and supporting ability. This may occur especially in women who already have preexisting weakened pelvic-supporting structures from childbirth. It expresses itself in the bulging downward of the bladder (cystocele), the rectum (rectocele), or the dropping of the uterus (uterine prolapse).

Why So Many Symptoms Exist

It seems incredible that there can be such a variety of symptoms resulting from estrogen deficiency. The reason has to do with "estrogen receptors" in various organs throughout the body, including the ovaries, uterine lining, vagina, external genitalia, the brain, urinary tract, skin, bone, and blood vessels.

Estrogen receptors can be thought of as locks and estrogen as the key. When the key is in the lock, that particular organ or tissue is programmed to respond in a hormonally specific way. For example, when estrogen finds its way to its receptors in the vaginal lining, the vagina wall becomes thickened and well lubricated. Without estrogen, the receptors lie empty and dormant, resulting in a thinning of the vaginal wall and creating dryness and painful intercourse.

In other words, estrogen is a key to the way many parts of a woman's body operate. As levels of the estrogen "key" decline, many organs and tissues in a woman's body do not function in the way they were programmed.

HORMONE REPLACEMENT THERAPY

Hormone replacement therapy (HRT) is the replacement of the body's estrogen and progesterone that menopause has depleted. The next chapter is devoted entirely to HRT. You will see not only why two hormones are used but that the benefits of hormone replacement are considerable. Under hormone replacement, most of the symptoms listed above disappear. Disturbances of the menstrual cycle can be controlled and regulated with HRT. Hot flashes, night sweats, and atrophic vaginitis disappear. Insomnia, fatigue, emotional symptoms, joint pains, and many urinary tract disorders are often, and sometimes promptly, improved by HRT.

Emotional symptoms tend to take a little longer to respond to estrogen—months, even years. This causes many women being treated to become discouraged. Some may even need to spend time with a support counselor who can suggest ways a person can cope with these symptoms while waiting for the estrogen to do its job.

Estrogen also offers long-term health protection by halving the risk of heart attack and preventing osteoporosis altogether.

It is easy to begin to think that estrogen is some sort of panacea. It is not. There is much to consider before one decides to fill a prescription for it. There are side effects, potential health risks, and certain contraindications. Moreover, there can be disappointments when ongoing situational stresses masquerading as menopause symptoms do not go away with hormone replacement.

In deciding whether HRT is for you, there are many important things to address. It is a decision only you ultimately can make, but it should be an *informed* choice, made with your doctor's help. We want you to have all the facts, accurate facts, before you make your decision. As you read on, you should be weighing the positives against the negatives, the benefits against the risks.

But keep in mind that menopause is part of something bigger—mid-life. While menopause may be a major player in a mid-life woman's discomfort, physically and emotionally, it is often not the only cause. The external stresses discussed in chapter 2 are almost an invariable backdrop in the life of a menopausal woman. That is why we present mid-life and menopause together. We don't believe the two can be separated. The one affects the other. Each impacts one's ability to cope with the other.

WOMEN WHO WILL HAVE THE LEAST TROUBLE WITH MENOPAUSE

Statistics show that 75 percent of all menopausal women have symptoms severe enough to seek medical guidance. Approximately half of these women experience menopausal symptoms so severe that they are desperate for help.

The question is often raised whether there is a kind of litmus test that will predict those who will have difficulty during the menopausal years. The answer is yes, but it is only a generalization.

For example, the women who handle menopause best are those who have taken time to learn about this important time of their life. Good self-esteem; a track record of dealing well with stress; many friends; lots of outside interests, including being active in their churches and communities; and good marriages with supportive mates are factors seen in women who tend to be less affected by the menopausal changes that are taking place in their bodies.

Also, women whose mothers managed their own menopause with relative ease tend to follow suit, suggesting some hereditary influences at work. This may be explained as well by similar temperaments or the cultural similarities they share.

On the other hand, women who have a poor self-image or have a past history of difficulty in coping with stress do not seem to fare as well during menopause. Similarly, women who have histories of becoming emotional when their estrogen levels drop off, such as before their period (premenstrual syndrome) or immediately following childbirth (postpartum "blues") seem to be more vulnerable to menopausal symptoms. One thing is clear—some women are more sensitive to changes in their blood estrogen levels than others.

RECOGNIZING THE ONSET OF MENOPAUSE

You would think that since menopause is the most consistent event of mid-life, it would be easily recognized. But that is not always the case. In fact it often sneaks up on a woman before she even realizes it.

Menopausal symptoms usually begin sometime during a woman's forties, long before her final menstrual period. Occasionally they can appear even earlier. We even see some women beginning menopause in their thirties. So spouses and family members who expect "good old Mom" to go through menopause during the traditional fifties may be in for a rude awakening when suddenly at age forty-two she starts exhibiting mood swings.

Certain clues surface that suggest the onset of menopause. More often than not, emotional symptoms appear first—irritability, anxiety, depression, mood changes, emotional outbursts, crying for no reason, difficulty remembering, low self-esteem, feeling unloved and unappreciated, and diminished interest in sex.

Often a woman "going through the change" begins to behave in a way that is just not "like her." She may or may not be aware that anything is wrong. Sometimes she can be so emotionally charged that if someone even subtly points out her altered behavior, she may become defensive and strike out angrily at the observer, accusing him or her of exaggerating the situation.

I recommend that when a woman turns forty, she gather her family (or close friends if she is alone) around her. Together they should agree to be vigilant and attentive to any suggestion of menopausal symptoms during the next ten to fifteen years of her life. Any display of menopausal symptoms, physical or emotional, should then be brought to the woman's attention. This pact then requires the woman to go see her doctor upon the recommendation of family members. Most women welcome this support of loved ones and will follow through. These women are facing their mid-life and menopause responsibly.

FOUR

❧

Hormone Replacement
Therapy

AS we have discussed, during the premenopausal years there is a slow but steady decline
in estrogen production. This often leads to both
physical and emotional symptoms that can be
distressing for women. The good news is that
today's woman has many more options to
choose from in managing both mid-life and
menopause than her mother did years ago.

It is important to point out here that a woman
can be a victim of menopause long before her
final menses—a concept most people, including doctors, have trouble understanding. This
is unfortunate because many women who have
menopausal symptoms but who are still having
their periods won't go to their doctors to see if

they are in menopause. A woman does not have to stop having periods or suffer drenching night sweats to qualify for menopause and medical attention!

ESTROGEN

Fortunately, more and more of this country's primary care physicians—internists, family practitioners, obstetricians, and gynecologists—realize the newly discovered medical benefits of estrogen besides its ability to treat menopausal symptoms. Doctors are becoming increasingly more comfortable and confident in prescribing it as its safety becomes statistically established.

Confidence in and the increasing use of estrogen has come about largely because of the protective influence of cotherapy with progesterone.[1] Together they are referred to as hormone replacement therapy (HRT). When estrogen is used by itself, as in the case in which a woman has had a hysterectomy, hormone replacement is referred to as estrogen replacement therapy (ERT).

Almost all the estrogen being used in this country as part of HRT is "natural," meaning it comes from a natural source or its chemical formula is identical to hormones made in the body (see chapter 14, question 17). The most commonly prescribed estrogen in the U.S. (70 to 80 percent) is conjugated estrogen (Premarin), a pill derived from pregnant mares' urine; hence the name Premarin. It is my personal preference—not because we own Wyeth-Ayerst stock (we don't) but because Premarin has a time-tested, fifty-year track record. It is also available in many different strengths, making slight dosage alterations easier. Other types of estrogen marketed in the U.S. are pills (Estratab, Estrace, Ogen, and Ortho-Est); skin patches (Estraderm); injectables (Depo-estradiol and Delestrogen); and vaginal creams (Premarin, Estrace, Ogen, and Dienestrol). Each manufacturer claims advantages to their preparation, and it may be true that some forms of estrogen work better in various areas of the body because of varying affinity to receptor sites.

PROGESTERONE

Estrogen receptors seem to be located in most every part of the body, including the uterus. Too many "occupied" estrogen receptors in the uterus may cause excessive cellular activity in the uterine lining (called the endometrium) and may lead to a precancerous condition called endometrial hyperplasia. Progesterone is the agent that discourages this kind of activity from taking place both by ensuring a more complete slough of the uterine lining at the time of menses as well as decreasing the number of estrogen receptors in the lining cells.[2] This is the reason why progesterone should be used along with estrogen when at all possible in the woman who still has her uterus.

Prescribing progesterone along with estrogen for patients who have had a hysterectomy is still a bit controversial. But most physicians don't. When the uterus has been removed, there is no need for progesterone's protective effect on the endometrium. However, many authorities believe progesterone should be added if there is a personal history of osteoporosis, endometrial cancer, or endometriosis.

The oral progesterone most often used today in this country is called "progestin," or sometimes referred to as "progestogen." Progestins are a synthetic form of progesterone. That means they are made in the lab and have a slightly different chemical composition than does the progesterone made by the body's ovaries. The most commonly prescribed progestins in the United States are medroxyprogesterone acetate (Provera, Cycrin, and

Amen) and norethindrone (Aygestin, Norlutate, Micronor, and Nor Q D). The latter two products are packaged as a very low dose, progestin-only birth control pill.

The problem with synthetic progesterone is that about one in three women experience significant side effects similar to the premenstrual syndrome, i.e., fluid retention, irritability, depression, breast tenderness, and abdominal bloating. Most of the time these side effects are dose related, meaning their undesired symptoms can be minimized by keeping the progestin dosage low.

In some patients the premenstrual-like side effects can be alleviated with a diuretic. I prefer spironolactone (Aldactone) 25–50 mg/day for the last seven to ten days of progestin therapy.

Dr. Howard Judd of UCLA will give the progestin for fourteen days *but* just every three months. He states that this still protects the uterine lining while reducing the annoying progestin side effects by two thirds.

If synthetic progestins persist in causing too many undesired symptoms, I have found the natural form of progesterone to be a very suitable substitute. Though not yet officially approved by the Food and Drug Administration

(FDA) for mass manufacturing, some pharmacies will specially prepare this natural form of progesterone for you with a doctor's prescription. It can also be ordered from Women's International Pharmacy in Madison, Wisconsin (1-800-279-5708). This form of progesterone is micronized, a process designed to enhance its absorption from the bowel. It seems to protect the uterine wall just as effectively as its synthetic counterparts. I predict the natural form of progesterone, which is identical to that being made by the ovaries, will soon receive the FDA's unrestricted endorsement for manufacturers to produce.

Some opponents of HRT have pointed out that progestin negates or blunts the beneficial effect estrogen has on cholesterol metabolism (see chapter 5, Estrogen and the Cardiovascular System). Recent studies by Daniel R. Mishell, Jr., M.D., chairman of U.S.C. Medical Center's Department of Obstetrics and Gynecology, have failed to see this effect in the dosages we now normally use in HRT. Keeping the dosage of progestin low reduces the likelihood of side effects, but if the dosage gets too low, some unwanted bleeding may occur. Besides, any minor adverse changes in cholesterol that progestin could have may not be important anyway, since estrogen probably asserts the majority of its benefit directly on the arteries themselves.

Researchers are now investigating ways of getting the progesterone directly to the endometrial lining with vaginal rings or intrauterine devices. This really makes sense, for it would eliminate the general side effects. But I suspect the marketing of these devices is a long way off.

An occasional patient remains intolerant to all forms of progesterone because of side effects. In this situation it is medically permissible to stop progesterone cotherapy altogether and prescribe estrogen alone, often called "unopposed estrogen therapy." It is prescribed either daily, omitting the first five days of each month, or five days a week (skipping weekends). In either case monitoring for any unusual growth of the uterine lining (endometrium) is mandatory. This should be done once a year with either a vaginal ultrasound looking at the thickness of the endometrial lining or an office endometrial biopsy (a biopsy of the inside of the uterus). A slight increased risk of developing uterine cancer does seem to continue even after unopposed estrogens are stopped, however. This is one minor drawback to the plan.

Progestins can also help partially control hot flashes. This is important for women who can't take estrogen for whatever reason (see chapter 8, Alternatives to Estrogen).

BENEFITS OF HORMONE REPLACEMENT THERAPY

First, estrogen provides relief from the aggravating menopausal symptoms. In fact, today there is little reason for a mid-life woman to be forced to endure symptoms truly related to estrogen deficiency. They can be treated safely and simply with hormone replacement. Hot flashes should stop within days. The natural lubrication of the vagina is restored and maintained within a couple of weeks. It won't be long before the skin feels softer and smoother. Energy levels are likely to rise, and sleep patterns improve. Bone and joint pain will often subside. And emotional symptoms—if they are estrogen related and not due to ongoing situational stress—usually will lessen, though gradually. For many women estrogen is like a gentle tonic that restores them to a sense of well-being— permitting a more peaceful passage through this time of life.

Second, hormone replacement offers the opportunity to practice effective preventive medicine. The most exciting medical news today is that estrogen, which can enhance the quality of mid-life, may at the same time extend the quantity of life. Doctors now believe that hormone replacement therapy can increase longevity by reducing a woman's risk of developing osteoporosis, heart disease, and uterine cancer. One investigator has calculated that HRT imparts to its user an additional 2.6 quality mid-life years and not just extra years tacked on later in a nursing home.[3]

Estrogen and progesterone, when used together correctly in low doses, not only treat menopausal symptoms but can also actually help retard the aging process that affects the cardiovascular system and bones (see chapter 5, Estrogen and the Cardiovascular System, and chapter 6, Estrogen and Osteoporosis).

WHO SHOULD CONSIDER HRT?
There are four potential candidates for hormone replacement.

Candidate 1
This is the still-menstruating woman who is having menopausal symptoms and an FSH-confirmed diagnosis of menopause.[4] The blood FSH (see chapter 3, Understanding Menopause)

is an excellent and reliable test with which to diagnose menopause when a woman is still having periods. An important point to remember is not to have the blood sample drawn mid-cycle to avoid an erroneously high FSH that accompanies an occasional ovulation in the premenopausal years. I have my patients tested during or very soon after a menstrual period.

My wife (and coauthor), Mary, interviews all patients who come to the Menopause Center. She usually briefs me on the background of each person before I examine her. It gives me insight when I deal with the emotional and social aspects of patients who are having a particularly rough time getting through the mid-life years and menopause.

One premenopausal patient Mary interviewed is a perfect example of how hormones can help the mid-life woman. Mary tells the story:

"I'll be honest with you," Diane said. "I've come here to save my marriage."

Diane was forty-nine years old—attractive, blonde, well-dressed, and quite feminine. She was also straightforward and determined. She explained to me that she had just remarried four months earlier—to "the best-looking guy in the country. He looks like Kenny Rogers— beard and all."

Before I even got to her intake medical history, I was so curious that I asked what her problem was.

Diane leaned forward and said softly, "Sex. I can't do sex. And I'm going to lose him if I don't pull myself together."

As it turned out, her husband had been loving and patient with Diane, but in her mind she wasn't functioning like she should. She feared losing her only hope for happiness for the rest of her life.

I asked her to describe what was going on. "Well," she said, "in the preliminaries of lovemaking everything is pleasant, and I get really turned on. But then my mind begins to think about the pain I know is coming up, and I want to stop right there. Sex causes my vagina to hurt so much I just can't do it, and we both end up totally frustrated and unfulfilled. Then in the middle of the night I wake up drenched in sweat. I can tell you, I don't make a very attractive bed partner when I'm hot and sticky. This is really getting to me. What's happening?"

"Have you ever seen a doctor about this?" I asked.

"Yes," she replied. "But he said that because I'm still having periods, I couldn't be in menopause, and he wouldn't prescribe estrogen for me until I actually stopped my periods."

"I think we can help you," I replied. "If we find that you are actually in menopause and need estrogen, it will help with both your painful intercourse and the night sweats."

Diane's case was a bit unusual because vaginal dryness of this degree doesn't usually develop until after the periods have stopped altogether. But it can on occasion be an early and distressing symptom of menopause (yeast vaginitis must also be ruled out because it too causes vaginal dryness). At any rate, Diane's two problems were resolved in just a matter of a few weeks with oral hormone replacement and some vaginal estrogen cream. Later Mary got a postcard from her that said: "Dear Mary, On my second honeymoon. Everything is perfect! Diane."

Diane was premenopausal and had symptoms. She needed hormone treatment. But there are many premenopausal women with no symptoms. Even though their FSH may be elevated, they do not need to be treated. If they have sufficient endogenous estrogen to menstruate, they have sufficient estrogen to protect their heart and bones from the long-term complications of estrogen deficiency.

Candidate 2

The second candidate for hormone replacement is the one who experiences disturbing symptoms highly suggestive of menopause but whose FSH is "borderline"—close to but not quite meeting the laboratory criteria for menopause. This is the premenopausal individual with intermittent symptoms. For her a six-month trial of HRT is reasonable. If she notices a definite improvement in her symptoms during those months and wants to continue HRT on through the menopausal years, she should be permitted to do so. This kind of long-term hormone usage offers a bonus—she is able to avoid menopausal symptoms altogether.

Candidate 3

The third potential candidate for hormone replacement is one who has stopped her periods and is clearly postmenopausal (confirmed by FSH if any questions exist as to why she has stopped her periods). It should make no difference whether she is having menopausal symptoms or not. The rationale for her choosing HRT is primarily preventive health care—avoiding or reducing the possible long-term complications of inadequate estrogen, which can be cardiovascular disease, osteoporosis, and chronic vaginal dryness and painful intercourse. Notice I said, *can be*. Certainly not all women are going to develop these problems when they lose their estrogen production as a result of menopause or surgery, but many will.

Candidate 4
The fourth person who should consider hormone replacement is the woman who has had a hysterectomy—surgical menopause. In this instance, two considerations are of importance in determining the need for hormones. First is the age at which the surgery is performed, and second is whether the ovaries are removed at the time of the hysterectomy.

In a woman fifty years old or less, if only the uterus is removed, estrogen replacement is not necessary until she develops menopausal symptoms or her FSH blood level rises into the menopausal range, whichever comes first (see chapter 14, question 18).

Hysterectomy after age fifty, with or without removal of ovaries (in other words, close to when natural menopause would ordinarily take place), in a woman with few or no menopausal symptoms calls for a personal decision whether or not to start estrogen for its long-term cardiovascular and bone-protecting qualities (see chapter 7, A Matter of Choice—Yours).

DISADVANTAGES AND SIDE EFFECTS OF ESTROGEN

So far in this chapter I have presented just the positive aspects of estrogen. What are the negatives? What are the risks? There must be risks because no medication is 100 percent safe, not even aspirin. Hormone replacement is no exception.

Some studies show that estrogen users may have a higher incidence of gallbladder disease; other studies show no increased risk. But to be safe, if you are on HRT, you should report any gallbladder symptoms, such as pain or persistent indigestion, to your doctor.

Some have listed as a disadvantage that, once started, HRT must be continued for life. I tend to disagree, though conceding that if and when estrogen is discontinued, the process of osteoporosis could resume at the same pace as before the estrogens were started. But at that time a bone density test may indicate that you are not at risk for developing osteoporosis during the remaining years of your life. Moreover, your cardiovascular situation may not be in jeopardy either. I do not personally think that, once started, a person is committed to HRT for the rest of her life.

Some women on HRT may experience breast tenderness, fluid retention, mild weight gain, irritability, or other premenstrual-like symptoms. They can range from mild to severe. More often than not the culprit is the progesterone. Usually with minor adjustments in dosage or substitution with other progesterones, these symptoms can be stopped or at least minimized.

Irregular bleeding not infrequently accompanies HRT when first started. It usually stops within a few months. However, if it persists and does not respond to adjustments in the dose or type of hormone, it might be necessary to undergo an office biopsy of the uterus (endometrial biopsy) or hysteroscopy, a periscopelike device used with local anesthesia that looks directly into the interior of the uterus. Both procedures mean additional expense.

Another disadvantage of hormone therapy is its cost, not an insignificant factor, especially when one considers long-term use.

The prices of estrogen and progesterone, of course, vary from pharmacy to pharmacy and depend on the quantity purchased. For example, a six-month supply of estrogen will be less expensive than buying a one-month supply.

Then there is the question of whether the hormones are covered by insurance. The cyclic method of HRT, which uses estrogen daily and progesterone for ten to twelve days a month, will cost on the average a little over twenty dollars per month.

The daily method of HRT will cost about ten dollars more. Vaginal estrogen cream, sometimes used alone or in conjunction with HRT, adds an additional twelve dollars per month. Keep in mind these are 1993 prices and very approximate. For the sake of comparison, women on birth-control pills now pay about twenty-two dollars a month for an average brand-name pill.

WOMEN WHO SHOULD NOT TAKE ESTROGEN

There are certain women who should *not* take estrogen:

1. Women who are pregnant or planning pregnancy.
2. Women who have undiagnosed vaginal bleeding.
3. Women suspected of having breast cancer or who have actually had it in the past (see chapter 9, Breast Cancer Patients and Estrogen).

4. Women with *active* vascular thrombosis (for example, blood clots in the legs or lungs). Note that most experts today agree that a past history of significant phlebitis (inflammation of the leg veins, with its potential to throw blood clots to the lungs) is no longer considered a contraindication to HRT *unless* the event took place while that person was on hormone replacement or birth-control pills at the time. Unlike contraceptives, low-dose HRT does not alter blood clotting factors in a clinically significant way.

Another theoretical contraindication to the use of hormones is clouded by some disagreement. It applies to someone who has an immediate family history of breast cancer—sister, mother, aunt, etc. In reviewing the literature we are on solid ground by saying, *if* you have a close family history of breast cancer, there *is* an increased risk of developing breast cancer. But the largest and best studies fail to show that this risk is further increased with the use of estrogen replacement. Therefore, I prescribe HRT to my patients who have a family history of breast cancer as do many clinicians I consider experts on the subject, such as Drs. Speroff, Stampfer, and Nachtigall.

BEFORE STARTING HRT

Before beginning HRT there are a few precautions that one should observe:

1. The thyroid gland should be tested. Low thyroid can cause symptoms similar to menopause.
2. It should be determined that one is not pregnant.
3. If there has been any abnormal bleeding, it must first be investigated.
4. There should have been a breast exam and mammogram within the past year.

HOW ARE HORMONES TO BE TAKEN?

There are many different ways to take estrogen and many different brands. There are pills (Premarin, Estrace, Ogen, Estratab, and Ortho-Est), skin patches (Estraderm), vaginal cream (Estrace, Premarin, Ogen, and Dienestrol), and injections (Delestrogen and Depo-Estradiol). Other sources such as subcutaneous pellets, skin gels, and vaginal rings may be available in the future but are now only being used on a research basis.

The Cyclic Method

If you are still menstruating regularly, it is best to work with your own cycle and not try to override it as in the case of the "daily method" (see below). To persist is only asking for frustrating irregular bleeding. It is far better for younger menopausal women to take estrogen and progesterone in such a way as to have planned, regularly induced monthly periods. This is called the cyclic method of giving HRT. Each hormone is started on designated days during the cycle counting from day "one." This could be your first day of flow or the first day of the calendar month. Estrogen is started on day one and taken for twenty-five days. The progestin is added to it during the last ten to twelve days. At that point both the estrogen and progestin are stopped for five days, inducing a period during the hormone free days. This same scheduling resumes again the next month.

Another method of cycling and one that I use frequently was introduced to us by our British colleagues. It has become very popular here in the U.S. because of its simplicity and ease. Using this method, estrogen is taken daily 365 days per year. To this is added one of the progestins on the first twelve days of the month— using the calendar. Actually, any twelve days can be chosen, and a shift is often necessary to get in sync with one's own cycling system of hormones when still partially at work.

The drawback of the cyclic method of HRT are the periods. This "inconvenience" has led to a far more acceptable regimen called the daily method.

The Daily Method

If you are like most women, you would like to stop having periods as soon as possible. The prospect of buying tampons at the drugstore at age seventy is hardly appealing. It is not only cruel to force postmenopausal women to have periods with HRT if they don't want them but totally unnecessary!

The daily method entails the use of one estrogen and one progesterone pill taken together each day, 365 days a year.[5] Some doctors prefer a Monday through Friday schedule, avoiding the weekends. The five-day method does seem to be accompanied by fewer side effects such as bleeding, breast tenderness, and bloating. About one-half of women starting off on either of these "daily" methods can expect some irregular spotting or bleeding for several months. But after that it is clear sailing, for most. For my patients who continue to bleed or spot beyond six months I prefer to perform a hysteroscopy in the office to identify such benign culprits as fibroids or polyps. It amazes me how often we find them. They are easily treated (without hysterectomy), thus enabling our patients to continue on with long-term hormone therapy without major surgery.

Use of the "daily" method affords one great advantage: It permits postmenopausal women to enjoy all the benefits of estrogen but without the periods. If you are postmenopausal and your doctor has you on cyclic HRT that causes periods, ask him if he would consider prescribing for you the more simple and convenient daily plan.

Giving estrogen daily is not only safe—it makes sense! In the past it was customary to stop HRT for five days each month—usually the first five days. It was thought that this would mimic the natural cycling system of the body. However, we now know that the ovaries don't "take a break" from producing estrogen during a woman's period. Therefore, there is no reason for the estrogen user to "take a break" either. The only exception to this is the occasional patient who, because she cannot tolerate any form of progesterone, is permitted to use estrogen alone (unopposed estrogen). A "break" either on weekends or the first five days of the month is probably safer for her.

There are many different and acceptable

methods of giving HRT. It is always best to tailor it to an individual's needs. If you decide to begin HRT, some fine-tuning adjustments may need to be made to achieve the best and most comfortable regimen. So don't give up if one method doesn't work. Work with your doctor to find the best program for you.

The estrogen skin patch (Estraderm) is another method of giving estrogen. It is especially good for women who don't seem to absorb oral estrogens well from their gastrointestinal tract. These "nonabsorbers" are those who are taking their oral estrogen faithfully but who continue to manifest menopausal symptoms. These individuals can be easily identified by a blood test called *estradiol* drawn twenty-four hours after ingestion of the last estrogen pill. If the estradiol is found to be low, this identifies the problem as an absorption one. The pill goes into the mouth but does not get into the bloodstream where it does its job. The solution is to bypass the bowel via skin patches or injections—the so-called nonoral methods.

Finally, when it comes to hormones, my advice is to avoid generics. Use brand-name products. At a January 1988 Boston meeting of the American College of Obstetricians and Gynecologists, evidence was presented confirming that generic hormones can be as much as 30 percent subpotent and, therefore, not equivalent to their brand-name counterparts. (See chapter 14, question 13 for more information about generics.)

FIVE

Estrogen and the Cardiovascular System

WOMEN rarely have heart attacks before menopause.

This observation has prompted researchers
to investigate the link between estrogen deficiency and arteriosclerosis. What virtually
every research study has shown is, I believe,
the greatest public health discovery in recent
decades—estrogen significantly reduces a
woman's risk of developing cardiovascular
disease.

In fact, women who take estrogen have approximately 40 to 50 percent fewer fatal heart
attacks and probably strokes than women who
do not take it.[1] It has been estimated that the
lives of approximately two hundred thousand

women could be saved each year if they just reduced their dietary fat and took estrogen.[2]

Hormone replacement probably provides this cardiovascular protection through estrogen's natural ability to improve the cholesterol levels in blood. However, a direct action of estrogen on the vessel wall may also be discouraging cholesterol plaques from being deposited there. This mechanism of protection may be playing an even *more* important role than lipid improvements.

CHOLESTEROL AND CARDIOVASCULAR DISEASE

When we speak of cardiovascular disease, we refer to diseases of the heart and blood vessels. The vessels of prime importance are the coronary arteries that serve the heart and the cerebral arteries that serve the brain. Blockage, or occlusion, of the coronary arteries leads to heart pain (angina) and heart attacks (myocardial infarction). Blockage of the cerebral arteries can lead to strokes.

Arteriosclerosis is a term referring to any process that causes the arteries to thicken and lose their elasticity. When the inner walls of the arteries thicken to the point that the channel (lumen) closes, oxygen-rich blood can't reach the vital organ it serves. By far the most common "coating" agent of the arteries is the yellow, waxy cholesterol plaque called atheroma. These scalelike deposits consist of cholesterol and other fatty material. Hence the term *atherosclerosis,* which is a more specific description of arteriosclerosis.

Nearly 70 percent of cholesterol is made in the liver. The rest comes into our body from food. Cholesterol is a lipid (fat) and is an important substance in meeting the needs of the body. For example, it helps to build healthy cells, and it serves as a building block from which all important hormones are made. Cholesterol circulates in our bloodstream "bundled" in a protein "package." The two together are called *lipoproteins* (*lipo* means "fat" and refers to cholesterol, and *protein* is the transporting vehicle in which the cholesterol is carried).

But here is an example of having too much of a good thing, for excess cholesterol in the body will form plaques on arterial walls much like corrosion building up in water pipes.

The unfortunate part of this is that the arteries of our body are coated with cholesterol silently. Our first suggestion of serious atherosclerosis is often a heart attack or stroke.

Our blood cholesterol is largely determined

by our lifestyle—what we eat, whether we smoke, our activity levels, and the degree of stress in our lives. It is also significantly influenced by hereditary factors, which are, of course, beyond our control. Now there is another factor we have to consider—estrogen.

TOTAL CHOLESTEROL
Aside from the health and life span of our parents, there is probably no greater predictor of one's longevity than cholesterol level. The so-called normal ranges used for cholesterol in the past have largely been abandoned. Instead, we now use ideal or preferred levels. The goal for every mid-life woman should be to keep her total cholesterol between 160 and 200. When it creeps above 240, it is too high, and when it exceeds 280, it is serious enough to consider cholesterol-lowering drugs if a restrictive diet has not helped.

CHOLESTEROL COMPONENTS
The total cholesterol value is only part of the picture. The cholesterol components are now broken down into "good guys" and "bad guys."

High-density lipoprotein cholesterols (HDL-C) are the "good guys," the protectors, for they sweep away dangerous plaque buildup. Women should have as their goal to keep their HDL-C as high as possible, for example over 55, but the higher the better. Some call them the "healthy" cholesterol element or the "highly desirable" ones (referring to the *H* and *D* in high density). Women usually have much higher HDL-C levels than men, and that is why it is rare for women under age fifty to have heart attacks. However, the HDL-C "blessing" is removed after menopause when estrogen is lost. After that the cardiac risk of women approaches that of men. HDL-C is mostly governed by hereditary factors, but it can also be raised through exercise, weight loss, and estrogen therapy. In contrast, it is suppressed by menopause's estrogen reduction, obesity, sedentary lifestyles, and smoking (including secondhand smoke).

HDL-C is so important in its protective role that even when a woman's total cholesterol level drifts above the magic 200 mark, I don't rap her on the head with a cholesterol diet book if her HDL-C is in the high range.

Recently, researchers have further subdivided HDL-C into HDL$_1$-C and HDL$_2$-C, finding the latter is probably the one that confers the lion's share of the vessel's wall protection.

On the other hand, low-density lipoprotein cholesterols (LDL-C) are the "bad guys." I remember them as the "lousy" cholesterols or the "least desirable" (referring to the L and D in low density). Low-density lipoprotein cholesterols are the silent killers. They do the damage by depositing themselves on the walls of arteries. Elevated LDL-C increases a person's risk of both heart attack and stroke. For best health, the mid-life woman should keep her LDL-C under 130. Anything over 160 is too high. LDL-C is influenced largely by diet and estrogen, things that we do have control over.

Every mid-life woman should know what her cholesterol profile is and have it rechecked every one to five years, depending on its level. This blood test should be done after a twelve-hour fast. The total cholesterol alone is not enough. It is important to know the value of its components. Total cholesterol—triglycerides (very low-density lipoprotein cholesterol seen elevated in a special type of hereditary lipid disorder), high-density lipoprotein cholesterol, and low-density lipoprotein cholesterol—makes up what we call the cholesterol "panel" or profile. Many labs will calculate a risk ratio that compares the various components of total cholesterol to each other, permitting one to compare their actual risk of having a heart attack with others their age.

To achieve the desired goal of total cholesterol between 160 and 200, a HDL-C greater than 55, and a LDL-C of less than 130 means keeping one's diet low in cholesterol and saturated fats. It means regular exercise at least three times a week (brisk walking for at least thirty minutes can do wonders not only for cholesterol but also for a relationship!). And if you choose, a tailored plan of hormone replacement (see chapter 4, Hormone Replacement Therapy).

Let me offer a word about diet and medication before discussing the role of estrogen in lipid metabolism. We Americans just plain eat too much fat—especially saturated fat. But simple readjustments made in the diet pay big cardiovascular dividends and all without disrupting our lifestyle. Our life expectancy is intimately related to two things: hereditary factors (over which we have no control) and our cholesterol level (which we can control). So it makes good sense to be conscientious about our cholesterol and lifestyle habits. It may be even *more* important for women than men because women who develop coronary artery disease probably have a worse prognosis than men.[3]

When a patient comes to the Menopause

Center with a cholesterol profile that concerns me, I often recommend Dr. Robert Kowalski's best-selling book, *The 8-Week Cholesterol Cure* (Harper & Row, 1987). In a straightforward and easy-to-read manner, he teaches the reader how to keep fat intake down and how to use bran and timed-release niacin to lower blood cholesterol by 40 percent. Though his niacin recommendations have been criticized as being too high, that certainly should not take away from the value of the book's dietary principles; his niacin dosages and schedule can be individually revised downward. His program does work. Whether it's the result of fat reduction, bran, niacin, or all three is not known. When I saw my own cholesterol drifting up, I put his claim to the test and was able to lower my cholesterol by 35 percent (even with a little "cheating"). So it does work, but like any dietary program, one must stay with it! Another informative book is *Good Fat, Bad Fat—How to Lower Your Cholesterol and Beat the Odds of a Heart Attack* by Glen C. Griffin and William P. Castelli (Fisher Books, 1989).

Each percentage point is critical. For every one-point drop in cholesterol there is a corresponding 2 percent reduction in the risk of heart attack.

If, however, a woman with significantly elevated cholesterol is unable to reduce it to reasonable levels with diet and niacin, she should be considered for one of the cholesterol-lowering drugs by her doctor. Keeping our cholesterol level under control is just that important!

CARDIOVASCULAR BENEFITS OF ESTROGEN

More than thirty studies to date have shown that postmenopausal use of estrogen protects against coronary artery disease. Through hormone replacement, a woman's total blood cholesterol will fall, the "healthy" cholesterols (HDL-C) rise, and the "lousy" cholesterols (LDL-C) decrease—just what she wants. But there are now animal studies to indicate that a major portion of estrogen's protective action on the cardiovascular system may be mediated through a direct effect on the blood vessels themselves where researchers now think they have found estrogen receptors. This means that even those women with enviable cholesterol levels can expect protection via this direct mechanism.

For women, the cardiovascular benefits of hormone replacement translate into a longer, more comfortable, and more productive life.

(It is unfortunate that men, who are at much higher risk than women, cannot enjoy the benefits of estrogen. But the side effects for men—breast development, decreased libido, and a higher voice—exact too high a price. Years ago researchers gave estrogen in high dosages to men who had had a heart attack. The experiment was terminated when it was found that it only made their cardiac situation worse. To my knowledge, no study has been done giving estrogen in very low doses to men to see if it would improve their cholesterol status without appreciable side effects.)

It is especially important for women who have high blood pressure or diabetes to be on hormone replacement therapy. In past years these conditions were considered a reason not to take hormones. No longer. Patients with high blood pressure, diabetes, and those with known coronary artery disease are the very ones who need the cholesterol-improving benefits that estrogen offers.

Cholesterol is something we all should be serious about. It kills. For women, estrogen helps to hold this dangerous killer in check.

SIX

Estrogen and Osteoporosis

OSTEOPOROSIS, a term that means "porous bones," can be one of the most serious medical problems facing a woman as she grows older. This often painful and disabling bone disorder eventually afflicts 40 percent of American women—all because of the loss of ovarian function. Whether surgical or natural, menopause leads to a decrease in bone mass and a corresponding increase of fracture risk.

During a woman's fifties and sixties, as her estrogen level becomes drastically reduced, she can lose up to 30 percent of her total skeletal mass. But the most accelerated bone loss takes place during the first five years following her final menses or surgical removal of the ovaries.

Because the process of osteoporosis takes place silently, the first suggestion of its presence is often a disabling fracture. Unfortunately, by the time osteoporosis is first seen on a standard X-ray film, extensive bone damage has already taken place. However, it now can be detected much earlier with the use of special bone density testing.

Osteoporosis is an insidious bone disorder in which calcium is stripped from the bones, leaving them thin, brittle, and easily broken. The bones most often affected and most susceptible to fractures are the hip, vertebral bones of the spinal column, and the wrists.

Unsteadiness that comes with old age often results in serious falls. For younger people, an unexpected topple may leave only a telltale bruise. But when the victim's bones are already weakened from osteoporosis, the result can be a catastrophic event as in the case of hip fractures.

HIP FRACTURES

A woman who breaks her hip actually has a 20 percent chance of dying from its medical complications. Women who do survive are too often left helpless invalids. I recall a medical school professor who, emphasizing the seriousness of this kind of injury, once quipped, "We enter this life through the pelvis and leave by way of the hip."

Not only are hip fractures disabling, they are also expensive. Some researchers estimate that hip fractures alone cost our nation more than $5 billion a year just in acute medical care.

VERTEBRAL FRACTURES

Multiple, often painless, fractures of the vertebral bones of the spinal column lead to the classic picture of osteoporosis. We've all seen this victim—the elderly lady supporting herself with a cane, hunched over, trying to get through life gazing up from a bent-over, unnatural position. The unsightly deformity of her upper back is called the dowager's hump. It develops as vertebrae of the spinal column collapse upon each other from tiny, recurring fractures and their accompanying loss of bone mineral. The average American woman shrinks an inch and a half each decade of life after the age of fifty as the result of these small crush fractures.

WRIST FRACTURES

The wrists are the third most common site of osteoporosis fractures in women. Known medically as Colle's fracture, they are incurred as an older person, realizing she is falling, instinctively reaches out to break the fall—instead she breaks her wrist. For young people a Colle's fracture is a rather minor event that mends in six weeks, but for the elderly it can be disabling for a long time.

NEEDLESS SUFFERING

Let me give you an example of what the ravages of osteoporosis can do to a senior citizen.

Early one morning as I walked from the parking lot to my office, I looked up to see a tiny figure dressed in a polyester print dress walking slowly ahead of me.

There's Bernice coming in for her annual checkup, I thought to myself.

Bernice has been my patient for nearly eighteen years. She is seventy-eight now. She came out of an era when women were forced to persevere through menopause without estrogen. Every time Bernice visits my office, I see in her face years of needless pain and suffering. She's already been hospitalized twice with hip fractures; her spine is nearly doubled over. Bernice uses a walker to get around. Many times she has shared with me the frustration she feels having to depend so much on her family and friends to accomplish even the simplest of tasks.

"I guess I don't mind the pain as much as I used to," she confided to me one day. "Maybe I'm getting used to it. But the biggest disappointment is not being able to do things with my grandchildren."

Not many years ago when researchers established the relationship of osteoporosis and estrogen, I put Bernice on estrogen and calcium supplements. It helped some, but the long-term damage was already too extensive. Years without estrogen had taken their toll.

Today's women can avoid the crippling years that Bernice has had to endure.

THE ANATOMY OF OSTEOPOROSIS

Bone is composed of a protein lattice work called the matrix. Calcium and other mineral salts are deposited on the matrix. That's what gives it its strength. It is a dynamic process—calcium constantly being added to or reabsorbed from this bone scaffolding.

During one's early years more calcium is deposited on the bone than is being reabsorbed. This accounts for the greater bone strength younger people enjoy. Maximum bone mass and sturdiness are usually reached in a person's mid-twenties. From that point on, more calcium is reabsorbed than added, leading to a gradual decrease in bone concentration at the rate of about one percent a year. Using electron microscopy it is possible to see the lattice beams becoming thinner, cracking, and even separating from each other.

Ninety-nine percent of our calcium is in bone, the body's great storehouse. When calcium and phosphorus enter our body from foods or supplements, they immediately enter the bloodstream where they are used by the cells of certain tissues. The rest are deposited in the bone.

BONES—OUR "BANK ACCOUNT"

I enjoy the way Dr. Bruce Edinger, clinical professor of medicine and radiology at the University of California at San Francisco and an expert on osteoporosis, describes the process of bone formation. He likens it to a "bank account." Most calcium "deposits" are made during the adolescent years. Most of the "withdrawals" are made later in life, especially during the first five years following menopause. Once 50 percent of the bone mass is lost, the skeleton becomes virtually "bankrupt" and unable to meet simple physical demands placed upon it.

Bone is a busy "bank" with deposits and withdrawals constantly and simultaneously being made. But the bank's top priority is keeping the blood level of calcium at a constant level. A delicate balance of calcium in blood and tissues is critical for proper cellular function (especially the muscle cells). In short, without calcium we could not live.

When our calcium intake gets reduced or its absorption from the intestines diminishes, the body must make more "withdrawals" from the (bone) "bank" to maintain normal blood levels.

When calcium concentrations in the blood get too high, the surplus is "deposited" back into the (bone) bank, which of course strengthens the skeletal system.

This explains why we must not only have adequate intake of calcium and phosphorus in our diet but also be able to absorb these mineral salts from the intestines, one of the tasks assigned to estrogen.

Two more important ways, however, in which estrogen prevents osteoporosis is by discouraging the reabsorption of calcium from the bone itself and by inhibiting the excretion of calcium through the urine. This makes estrogen the bone bank's chief executive officer!

BIG BONES, SMALL BONES

Both men and women lose bone mass as they age. As we get older we absorb calcium less efficiently. But bone loss affects women more than men because women, having smaller bones than men to begin with, cannot afford to lose as much bone without experiencing its serious consequences.

The principle of bone mass differences also explains why osteoporosis targets some people more than others. For example, women with small bone structures are more susceptible to osteoporotic fractures than are larger-framed women. Asians and Caucasians have a higher incidence of osteoporosis than do Afro-Americans for the same reason. In fact, osteoporosis in Afro-American males is almost nonexistent.

OTHER RISK FACTORS

There are other factors (hereditary, lifestyle, and dietary) that help us identify those high-risk individuals who are most susceptible to osteoporosis. Women whose mothers experienced hip fractures have an increased risk of developing osteoporosis. People who smoke (smoking reduces circulating estrogen), drink (alcohol probably has a direct toxic effect on bone), and those who are more sedentary or tend to have calcium-deficient diets are the ones at greater risk for osteoporosis.

The "ideal" osteoporosis candidate then is a woman who is small, either white or Asian, has a distaste for (or perhaps an allergy to) dairy products, refuses to take hormones and calcium supplements, has had an early menopause (either spontaneous or surgical), is a smoker and drinker, and has a mother who had a late-in-life hip fracture. The chance of this woman getting osteoporosis is virtually 100 percent.

Recognizing high-risk individuals is a giant step toward early detection and prevention. Remember, there is no cure for osteoporosis, but it can be prevented.

HOW TO AVOID OSTEOPOROSIS

Calcium

A recent government study showed that after age thirty-five, more than 75 percent of women in the United States have calcium intakes well below the 800-milligram recommended daily allowance (RDA).

With this in mind, and since bone loss begins

around age thirty-five, all women (especially those who are small boned) should be especially vigilant that their diet includes calcium and vitamin D–enriched foods. Unfortunately, this means taking in a lot of dairy products that can also be high in cholesterol. The way around this dilemma is for women to rely more heavily on calcium supplements.

Women whose diet is not adequate in calcium would be wise to take approximately 500 milligrams of extra calcium a day (the average amount of calcium in the daily diet of most women is about 500 milligrams) starting in their mid-thirties. This should be increased to 1000 milligrams of extra calcium a day as she approaches menopause and 1500 milligrams after menopause.

Many women believe that a high-calcium intake alone will protect them against osteoporosis. It won't. Estrogen is the key. However, taking calcium supplements is an important adjuvant because estrogen needs calcium to do its job of preventing osteoporosis.

It is important not to be misled or confused by all the advertising "hype" that goes on today about calcium. There are dozens of calcium supplements on the market. Most contain one of three calcium compounds: calcium carbonate, calcium lactate, or calcium gluconate. All seem to be adequately absorbed, but they differ in regard to the amount of elemental calcium in each.

For example, calcium carbonate, which is the least expensive of the three, has 40 percent calcium—the highest concentration available. By contrast, calcium lactate tablets have only 13 percent calcium, while the gluconates have just 9 percent. Obviously, the lower the percentage of actual calcium, the more pills must be swallowed each day, which also increases the cost. But in fairness to the calcium lactates and gluconates, they do seem to cause less constipation and gas than do the carbonates in some people. So it becomes an individual choice.

Two important points about calcium. One, when adding up the milligrams from the package, count only the milligrams of calcium and not the other associated compounds like carbonate, lactate, and gluconate. In the past, manufacturers have tried to lump them together, leading you to believe you are getting more milligrams of calcium than you actually are. Add up only the amount of elemental calcium. Second, take your calcium during meals and at bedtime in divided doses for better absorption.

A word about vitamin D. Vitamin D promotes

calcium absorption from the intestinal tract, but as a fat-soluble vitamin, it has the potential to build to toxic levels in the body. Even though most adults take in sufficient amounts of vitamin D through exposure to sunlight and dairy products, most experts advise taking 400 I.U. of vitamin D supplement along with the calcium every day. That amount is safe.

There may be a beneficial role of the mineral magnesium in increasing bone density. It has been proposed that those who are not on estrogen take 600 mg of magnesium per day (200 percent of the government's daily recommended allowance). However, as yet it is not being advocated by osteoporosis experts, probably because it has not been adequately studied.

Exercise

Weight-bearing exercise also helps to retard osteoporosis. By putting extra stress on the skeletal system, bone cells are encouraged to replace themselves. The bones stay dense and strong with exercise, provided there is adequate estrogen and calcium available. The mid-life woman should make time for brisk walking or even low-impact aerobics. Swimming and bicycle riding, though not weight-bearing exercises, are nontraumatic forms of aerobic exer-

cise that are not only good for the cardiovascular system but, because the muscles are attached to bone, also strengthen the total body
skeleton. All forms of aerobic exercise help
bones in another important way. They increase
a person's stability and reaction time, both of
which help avoid bone-breaking falls.

Densometry

Early detection of osteoporosis is possible with
special instruments called densometers or
absorptiometers. They are able to simply and
safely measure a person's bone mineral content. Some are designed for use on the wrist
bones, while others more accurately look at the
spine or hip. There is no one machine that can
assess our overall fracture risk by looking at
just one site. To determine the risk of hip fracture from osteoporosis one must examine the
hip joints densometrically. The same for the
spine or the arm. Probably the best state-of-the-
art equipment being used today for doing density studies is DEXA (Dual Energy X ray
Absorptiometer) because of its accuracy and
lowered exposure to X rays.

In our program we do not routinely order
bone-density tests but reserve them for those at
high risk or for those individuals who are un-

comfortable with the thought of taking hormones. In the latter instance, if the bone-density testing demonstrates unequivocal evidence of osteoporosis, we hope that person might reconsider her original decision.

However, some medical centers do routinely monitor all patients for osteoporosis before and after starting estrogen. I cannot argue with that approach, although it does impose an additional expense. Their rationale is that what appears to be an adequate dosage of estrogen may, in fact, not be enough. They feel a periodic follow-up with the densometer helps to target the occasional patient who may need a higher dose of estrogen. This would be much like a blood pressure recheck on a patient who has been started on high blood pressure medicine.

Hormone Replacement Therapy

There is no question that osteoporosis is directly linked to low estrogen. Therefore, for menopausal women who are losing their estrogen production, ensuring a constant source of estrogen is the best and first line of defense. Moreover, it appears that it is never too late to start estrogen therapy for its bone-improving effects, so no matter what your age, don't rule out estrogen therapy.

Osteoporosis specialist Morris Notelovitz, M.D., of Gainsville, Florida, warns, "Women who think they need not worry about calcium or estrogen because they exercise regularly could be sadly mistaken." He is reinforcing a fact—exercise cannot do what estrogen plus calcium can do.

It is also important to emphasize that estrogen is primarily a *preventive* measure, but it has been shown that when started in women over sixty, it will add 13 percent to bone density in just two years. Estrogen should always be seriously considered whenever osteoporosis is diagnosed. Research has also confirmed that estrogen when used with progestin encourages new bone to be deposited more effectively in sites where bone has been lost than estrogen alone.[1] This means that it is very possible to partially undo bone-loss damage already incurred. However, progestin alone will not accomplish this. It must work in concert with estrogen.

If someone wishes to use the lowest dosage possible of conjugated estrogen for whatever reason (lower than the .625 mg. recommended dose), it has now been shown that Premarin .3 mg/day plus 1500 mg of calcium/day will prevent bone loss in women *if* started within five years of their menopause.[2]

Non-Estrogen Drugs for Osteoporosis
There are now some very effective nonhormonal drugs available to treat osteoporosis once it has developed. Etidronate (Didronel) has the ability to create more bone-forming cells in the body. We have seen remarkable increases in bone mass with the use of Didronel.

Joan, an attractive blonde, middle-aged woman, had virtually no osteoporosis risk factors. She began having back pain. Her orthopedist, after reviewing her X rays, felt she was showing signs of osteoporosis. A bone-density test confirmed this. Highly unusual, we all agreed, since she had been on estrogen for a long time and exercised almost daily. She was not faithful, however, with her calcium intake. She was given Didronel, in the usual way, orally for fourteen days every three months and encouraged to take her calcium supplement regularly. Less than a year later a repeat densometry showed a 58 percent increase in her bone mass! The benefits of Didronel use beyond two years have not yet been studied, but I would expect the same continued benefit.

Calcitonin is another effective drug for osteoporosis, but it is very expensive and inconvenient, requiring daily injections. We are hopeful that a nasal spray form will be released this year. It works by discouraging the stripping of calcium from the bone matrix.

SEVEN

❧

A Matter of Choice— Yours

To take hormones or not to take hormones—that is the question.

If estrogen can do so much, why are only 15 percent of the country's postmenopausal women receiving estrogen replacement? Why is it that one-third of all patients who are given prescriptions for hormones never bother to fill them? Why do 20 percent of women stop taking their estrogen within nine months?

These are all profound questions and should give us all in the medical field pause to ask why. Is it a matter of doctors simply not taking the time to explain HRT more thoroughly? Is it restricted access to medical care to find treatment for menopause? Is it cultural differences in attitudes toward menopause? What explains this global lack of compliance?

I believe the number one reason is *fear*—fear that hormones may cause cancer. Every patient I talk to about HRT wants to first know, "Is it safe?" "Does it cause cancer?" No one feels comfortable taking hormones until these questions are resolved in their minds.

The cancer concern was spawned back in 1947 when researcher J. J. Bitter proposed the concept that excessive hormone stimulation increases the risk of tumors in animals.[1] The question was, does his hypothesis apply to humans? Does estrogen contribute to the development of cancer in humans?

In the sixties it seemed Bitter's postulation might be correct at least in regard to the uterus. During those years it became fashionable to prescribe estrogen for continued youthfulness. Women were enticed to their doctors' offices for massive amounts of estrogen in the form of shots and pills. At that time not enough research had been done and not enough thought given by doctors and scientists to keep estrogen dosages low and to use progesterone along with it to prevent excessive stimulation of the uterine lining.

In the seventies, some women who had

been taking estrogen, usually in high dosages and without the balancing influence of progesterone, developed a nonaggressive form of cancer of the uterus called endometrial cancer. Overnight women became wary of estrogen, and doctors, in turn, stopped writing prescriptions for it.

Then came speculation that if estrogen could provoke cancers in the uterus, could it do the same thing to the breast or other organs. Even though this speculation was false, the damage had already been done—the seed of doubt planted. Not surprisingly, this fear set the treatment of the menopausal woman's needs back many years. Once again the midlife woman was forced into an intolerable position of "gutting it out" through menopause with basically no medical help.

However, in the eighties things changed. Research into estrogen, its benefits and safety features, went into high gear. It started being prescribed only in low reasonable dosages and along with progesterone. By so doing, hormone therapy was prescribed in a manner as to mimic the *natural* hormone production of the body's ovaries in regard to its natural dosage, cycling, and chemical makeup. This commitment to keeping it "natural" has eliminated the risks of hormone replacement.

Still, many women continue to fear the use of estrogen because of those earlier scares surrounding endometrial cancer. Let's look at the facts.

UTERINE CANCER AND HRT

We now know that taking estrogen *alone* in high dosages and over a prolonged period of time increases the risk of developing uterine cancer—in fact, six cases per one thousand women per year. However, by taking progesterone along with estrogen, the risk of developing uterine cancer is only about one case per one thousand women per year—*less* than in women not using any hormones at all.[2] Therefore, in regards to uterine cancer, estrogen, when used with progesterone, not only *doesn't* cause uterine cancer—*it prevents it!*

BREAST CANCER AND HRT

At the time of this writing there are more than fifty-one epidemiological studies dealing with the relationship of estrogens to breast cancer. All have failed statistically to show that estrogen increases the risk of developing breast cancer, and *no* studies to date have shown any increase in the mortality rate from breast cancer by estrogen users, according to England's Dr. John Studd in his lecture before the North American Menopause Society in 1993. Even efforts to critically analyze the data by focusing on just the best and most acceptable studies, called meta-analyses, have failed to show a statistical relationship.[3] Many of the individual studies are large and impressive, such as the multidecade Nurses Health Study.[4]

Some studies show a slight increased risk of developing breast cancer in certain subgroups, while other studies show a slight decrease, sometimes in the very same subgroup. A "subgroup" is a special population within a study. Examples would be women who have had a positive family history of breast cancer, or women with the early onset of menstruation, or late menopause, late onset of first pregnancy, prolonged estrogen usage, obesity, drinking, smoking, or diets high in fats or low in fiber, etc.

Because of conflicting findings in some of the subgroups, many of us now feel that breast cancer appears to be a multifactorial type of cancer and ultimately will be found to depend far less on hormonal factors than on age, lifestyle, diet, environment, or family history of breast cancer.

Probably no subject has received as much research attention as the possible relationship between estrogen and breast cancer. One of the largest ongoing studies of HRT and breast cancer is by Dr. R. Don Gambrell, Jr., M.D., of Georgia.[5] Though many have criticized the mechanics of his study, it continues to show the same reduced incidence of breast cancer when women use estrogen and progestin together. Dr. Lila Nachtigall of New York has reported a twenty-two-year well-designed study in which there were seven cases of breast cancer in 52 patients who never used estrogen, whereas there were *none* in the 116 women who had used estrogen and progesterone together.[6]

These two studies do suggest that progestin added to estrogen could be reducing the risk of breast cancer. However, other investigators have not been able to confirm the impressive findings of these two investigators. A study called "PEPI" (Postmenopausal Estrogen Progestin Interventions Trial) is now being conducted at the National Institutes of Health in Washington, D.C., and scheduled for completion this year. We are all hoping it may shed more light on whether there is a protective role being played by progesterone on the breasts.

What do I think? I am personally concerned

to know why breast cancer continues to be on the rise. In 1940 only one in twenty American women fell victim to breast cancer. Today it is one in nine. The number of new cases is rising by 4.3 percent a year. Can this just be explained by the fact that women are living longer or that more frequent use of mammography is discovering tumors at earlier stages so that incidence figures appear higher? Probably not.

I am in total agreement with a man I have come to respect and admire very much. He has taught me much over the years. He is endocrinologist, writer, and lecturer Dr. Leon Speroff, chairman of the Department of Obstetrics and Gynecology at the University of Oregon, who has become known as the "father of hormone and menopausal medicine." Though very much a proponent of HRT, he appeals for caution. "We are asking women and their doctors to make a clinical judgment still without all the facts," he says. Dr. Speroff is right. We still need more *good* research on this subject. But my fear is that "all the facts" may lie outside the realm of hormone usage, in areas that have been only lightly studied. I think every attempt has been made from a research standpoint to implicate hormones in the increased incidence of breast cancer and has failed. Maybe the PEPI trial will be the "smoking gun," but I doubt it. I can't help but wonder about unknown environmental or lifestyle factors that we may be missing in our relentless pursuit to incriminate hormones as an inciting factor.

GOOD NEWS IN THE MIDST OF BAD

As I previously mentioned, statistics now indicate that one of nine women will get breast cancer during her lifetime. It is striking women who take hormones at the same rate as those who do not. But let's say you were one of the unfortunate "one in nine." Your chances of cure are *greater* if you are taking estrogen at the time of discovery. Three studies, in 1982, 1989, and 1992, looked at a sample of menopausal women.[7] In this group, when breast cancer did develop, the prognosis for those who were taking HRT was significantly much better than those who were not taking hormones at the time of the cancer's discovery. That *is* good news!

Until all the missing pieces of the puzzle are in place, however, women will be asked to make personal choices "without all the facts." In the meantime, I think women can find solace in one fact—*if* there is any increased risk of developing breast cancer from estrogen, *that risk is very, very small* and pales in comparison to the tremendous life-improving benefits estrogen affords both short and long term.

Fear of breast cancer is certainly the number one concern of women today as they decide what to do about hormones. But they also have other concerns that make them leery of taking hormones.

Bleeding

"I don't want to keep having periods, and I've heard that's what hormone therapy does." Yes, an HRT program can cause some undesired bleeding, but it all depends on what method you choose. If you are on the cyclic method (see chapter 4, Hormone Replacement Therapy), naturally it will mean continuing to have periods, but they will be regular and planned. If you are fortunate to be on the so-called daily plan, any unexpected bleeding will usually be short-lived.

Medical Warnings

Not just an occasional patient balks at taking her prescribed HRT because she is frightened by those scary information inserts included in the hormone package. The Food and Drug Administration (FDA) has been a good consumer watchdog over the years, but some people find the sometimes exhaustive list of real and potential risks a little overwhelming.

One severely menopausal woman came to us after being up four nights in a row because of night sweats. By the time I saw her, she looked totally exhausted. All she really needed was sleep, and that meant prescribing low-dose hormone replacement therapy. But she resisted. "A year ago a doctor prescribed some estrogen pills for me. When I got home and read the information brochure that came with the prescription, it scared me to death. I just threw the pills away."

Distrust of Male Physicians

Some women simply have a problem trusting male doctors who are telling them what they should be doing and not be doing with their bodies during menopause. *How can a man know what's going on inside me?* they ask themselves.

Well, it is really no different than a female physician who has never gone through menopause. How could she know? She might even be a little less sympathetic if she has never done personal battle with hormones and emotions. A male physician, on the other hand, has to call on experience and observation and may have less bias. Who knows? I guess it really depends on the doctor.

Unknown Long-Term Effects

Are there long-term consequences that will be discovered down the road? Women are still smarting about the DES (diethylstilbestrol) debacle of many decades ago. This "safe" synthetic estrogen was used to help prevent miscarriage. Later, however, not only was it shown to be ineffective but the drug also put daughters of DES patients in jeopardy of vaginal cancer and increased their risk of obstetrical complications. The likelihood of something similar to that happening today with such very low-dose natural estrogens is probably very remote, but whenever you take any chemical into your body, there are never any 100-percent guarantees in respect to its safety. The potential for down-the-road repercussions is always there and must be factored in on the risk side.

It's Not Natural

One patient asked me one day, "Since menopause is a natural event in the lives of women, isn't giving hormones interfering with God's plan for them?"

That is a valid concern, and I have personally grappled with it many times. Polio, smallpox, diphtheria, pertussis, and tetanus are all diseases that were once "natural," even commonplace. Fortunately, because of dedicated researchers, vaccines were developed to protect us from the ravages of those diseases. I believe God has given us skilled scientists for a reason and would want us to avail ourselves of their abilities.

The problem is that menopause is different because it is not a disease. Rather it is a natural process that takes place in a woman's body as a result of aging of the ovaries. Is there any other health example where it is "acceptable" to intervene in an attempt to forestall aging? I believe there is.

The heart's coronary vessels actually begin "aging" from birth. As the years go by, there is a slow but constant deposit of atherosclerotic plaques on the inner surfaces of these arteries. The rate of deposit, of course, varies from individual to individual. Actually one out of every two women will ultimately die from this aging process. So do we ignore it? Do we tell a woman who has angina (heart-induced chest pain) that, because her problem is part of the body's natural aging, we will not help her? Of course not. Every one of us, if we knew our coronaries were prematurely plugged, would want everything done to treat the problem, to extend the quality and quantity of our life. God has given us well-trained cardiologists and thoracic surgeons who use medications and operations to restore the health of those whose arteries have prematurely aged. In like fashion, I believe we *are* at liberty to treat and avoid the effects of aging ovaries. If we have something that will prevent the effects of estrogen deficiency, should we not use whatever medical science has to offer to avoid it and to extend and improve our life?

MAKING A DECISION IN PROPER PERSPECTIVE

The controversy to use or not use hormones will most likely continue to wage, but from the information available today it is the opinion of most physicians and scientists that estrogen does not cause breast cancer. Hormone replacement therapy is simply giving back to a woman hormones that she once naturally produced during her active reproductive years. I believe that fact alone makes hormone therapy as safe as her own ovaries.

Every mid-life woman should look at as many facts as she can about hormone therapy before filling a prescription. We encourage this because only when she sees that the benefits of HRT outweigh the risks will she feel totally comfortable taking hormones.

Based on her own personal research and feelings, each individual must make a decision that best fits her own personal needs. The decision may be yes; it may be no. But in either case, it should be an *informed* choice. As a decision is being made, there are three facts to keep in mind:

1. Menopause *does not* automatically call for the immediate replacement of hormones. In fact, there is no rush to make a decision. The ovaries do continue to produce estrogen even after the final menstrual period. However, the time taken to make that decision should be kept reasonable in view of the fact that most estrogen-related bone loss takes place during the first five years after menopause.

   Women who probably don't need hormones are those who go through mid-life with few if any menopausal symptoms. They are the ones whose mothers and father and grandparents all live to ripe old ages. They are women whose cholesterols are in the ideal range. They are the ones who exercise regularly and never miss taking their calcium supplements. Their bone density studies show virtually no bone loss. They don't smoke, drink, aren't too thin and may even be on the heavy side. Neither do they have any difficulty with intercourse because of vaginal dryness.

But there are far more less-disciplined women who are unable to develop the necessary health habits and lifestyle to manage menopause effectively. Physically and emotionally they are unable to cope with the changes menopause brings upon them. These women are thrilled to know that there is something available that can help them improve the quality and quantity of their life without disrupting it.

2. Estrogen offers significant benefits to its users. It offers relief from the symptoms of menopause that appear early: hot flashes, night sweats, insomnia, fatigue, joint pains, diminished libido, mood changes such as depression, anxiety, irritability, mental confusion, and memory loss.

3. Estrogen effectively provides long-term health protection from cardiovascular disease, osteoporosis, chronic vaginal dry-

ness, and uterine cancer when progesterone is used with estrogen.

Unquestionably some women will be frightened when a well-meaning friend whispers,
"Hormones cause cancer, you know." But keep
in mind that the issue is not simply the risks of
HRT; it also means considering the risks *without* HRT. Statistically, the greatest health risk to
a woman is not cancer but cardiovascular disease. Death from a heart attack is just as final
as death from breast cancer. But the thought of
breast cancer is more frightening and conjures
up a far more morbid picture than does a heart
attack or stroke.

Dr. Trudy L. Bush, associate professor of
epidemiology at Johns Hopkins University,
brings the whole issue into proper perspective
when she states:

> *Cardiovascular disease claims the lives of
> more American women than any other ill-
> ness. Risk factors for heart disease include
> age, race, hypertension, smoking, diabetes,
> and elevated lipids (cholesterols). Estrogen
> therapy reduces the risk of heart disease in
> women.*
>
> *When asked what health problem they*

most fear, the majority of women over forty years of age answer "breast cancer." Few mention cardiovascular disease as a major personal health concern. Yet statistics indicate that each year approximately 500,000 American women die from cardiovascular disease. Less than one tenth of this number die of breast cancer. When one considers lifetime risk, one of every two women will die from cardiovascular illness compared with one in eleven (nine) from breast cancer.[8]

Dr. Brian Henderson, of the USC School of Medicine, has confirmed these figures, summarizing them in the bar graph on page 142.

OUR CHOICE

The woman who suffers from symptoms of menopause or is concerned about her down-the-road health is the one who must ultimately decide if she wants (or needs) to receive estrogen's relief. Hopefully her decision will also take into consideration the advice and input from family and friends—the ones who must live with her.

I personally am convinced of the safety of HRT, convinced enough to prescribe it for my own wife, the one I love the most. It was *her*

HRT IN PERSPECTIVE

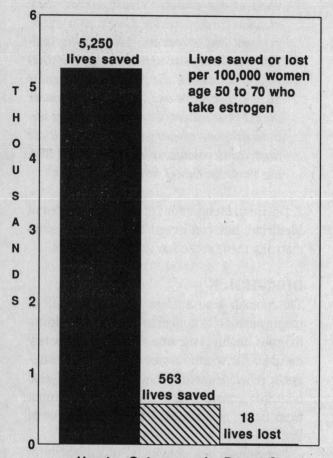

Lives saved or lost per 100,000 women age 50 to 70 who take estrogen

5,250 lives saved — Heart

563 lives saved — Osteoporosis

18 lives lost — Breast Ca.

Mod. Henderson et al, Am J Ob/Gyn 1986; 154: 1181

choice, but I felt then—and I still feel—at total peace with her decision to use HRT. And so does she.

For years Mary took the birth-control pill when it was considered controversial, and many at that time felt it was risky. But as it turned out, it was not the health hazard it was portrayed to be and is still considered safe even in older nonsmoking women for as long as they feel they need birth control. And what reassures me even more is the fact that the estrogen in the birth-control pill Mary once took was up to fifteen times stronger than the estrogen she now takes in HRT.[9]

Mary says, "I considered it carefully, read all the information I could get my hands on, listened to my husband [my doctor] talk about it, and thought it through carefully. I decided it was for me. I did have some concern about possible risks, but I was more concerned about preventing heart disease and osteoporosis. They both run in my family. Also, I didn't want to spend the rest of my life being limited and restricted by health problems that can be prevented. I've been on HRT for nearly nine years now and have not regretted it for one moment. For me, it has made a tremendous difference."

Obviously, Mary and I believe in the health-providing value of HRT. We see many women bravely enduring the difficulties of menopause when we know they don't have to. We know that hormones could improve the lives of many of these women now and later through their beneficial influence upon cardiovascular disease and osteoporosis. But at the same time, we are sympathetic to women who are overly cautious or who are concerned about whether or not this is "tampering with nature," or who are worried about any yet unsuspected future harm. Ultimately it ceases to be a matter of medical statistics and comes down to making a personal decision about one's own health and life.

Every woman must make her own decision, preferably in partnership with her doctor. Together they can decide whether to use hormones or not. And if not, there are alternatives. They are discussed in the next chapter.

❦

EIGHT

Alternatives to Estrogen

AT age fifty Betty had much to be thankful for. Nine years earlier she had been called back to the breast center for special views of her right breast. The telephone call terrified her. She had good reason. Magnification views were followed by a fine needle biopsy and the discovery of a very early breast cancer. After appropriate consultation, she opted to have a lumpectomy with removal of nearby lymph nodes (lymphadenectomy), followed by radiation therapy. All excised lymph nodes showed no cancer cells. The size of the cancer was very small, and her doctors considered her cured and told her so.

But she was miserable. Every night her sheets were drenched, she slept fitfully, and the next day it showed. Partially because of her hot flashes and night sweats and partially because of vaginal dryness, she and her husband Tom tacitly agreed to quit trying to have sex.

Betty went to her doctor. "Betty, the blood test I performed indicates you are definitely in menopause. Estrogen would significantly relieve your symptoms; I know that, but we've talked about this before. Because of the remote possibility estrogen might stimulate any hidden cancer cells, you could be putting yourself at undue risk by taking hormone replacement."

"But, doctor, I'm willing to take that chance. This is really affecting Tom and me. And I can tell you, our marriage is the most important thing in life to me. Those horrible menopausal symptoms are destroying our relationship. I'm willing to accept any risks there might be!"

Betty's doctor reluctantly wrote her out a prescription for estrogen. But he asked her to sign an informed consent and release of medical legal liability.

Estrogen usage in patients with a past history of breast cancer, regardless of how long it has been since the cancer was treated, its level of spread, or its receptor status, is forbidden by medical legal standards as determined by the FDA.

Betty's dilemma extends to other groups of women, too. Take, for example, the patients who have had phlebitis while on HRT or the birth-control pill (see contraindications in chapter 4, Hormone Replacement Therapy). Include another group, those who are too uncomfortable with the side effects of estrogen. And finally we can't forget the millions of women who have chosen not to go on hormones for whatever reason. We are talking about a lot of folks looking for nonhormonal alternatives. And there are alternatives.

If you are one who can't or won't take estrogen, here are the options available to you for the most common symptom of menopause— the hot flash—and those available to avoid the long-term complications of estrogen deficiency.

HOT FLASHES

Hot flashes and night sweats are possibly the most consistently distressing symptoms of menopause. If they could be diminished to tolerable levels, the passage through menopausal years would certainly be made easier. Dr. Fredi Kronenberg, Ph.D., assistant professor, College of Physicians and Surgeons, Columbia University, New York, offers some non-estrogen advice.

Dr. Kronenberg states that "in many cases, women can cope non-medically with their hot flashes if they have adequate information and support."[1]

That means first *educate* yourself about menopause and its management. Identify and avoid triggering events that often precede a hot flash—emotional stress, closed places, warm environment, caffeine, alcohol, things in your diet. Hot temperatures are frequent "triggers" that can be avoided by keeping your room cool. Wear clothing that has breathable natural fibers. Cotton sheets absorb perspiration and are more comfortable to the night-sweating victim. When they occur, take short deep breaths.

Second, reach out for *support*. Support groups are very helpful—talking with other women experiencing the same phenomenon is comforting. If no groups are immediately available, subscribe to newsletters of concerned organizations such as MidLife Women's Network, 5129 Logan Avenue, South Minneapolis, MN 55419-1019. Get counseling if you need to sort things out that are troubling you.

Make certain lifestyle changes when appropriate. *Stop smoking* (smoking lowers blood levels of estrogen being produced by your ovaries). *Exercise*. One Scandinavian study reported less severe flashes with exercise.[2]

PRESCRIPTION MEDICATIONS
There are some non-estrogen prescription drugs available—Bellergal, Catapres, Provera (oral or injections), Megace (a strong oral progestin)—that you can discuss with your doctor.

VITAMIN E
Dr. Kronenberg reports about 27 percent of her patients who took vitamin E felt the intensity and frequency of their hot flashes reduced. This is not much different than a placebo effect. But if you are one of the 27 percent, why not? The suggested dosage of vitamin E for hot flashes ranges from 300 to 1000 I.U./day.

HERBAL THERAPY
Herbs have long been used for the treatment of hot flashes. The Chinese have been using herbal remedies for centuries, individualizing treatment to achieve some remarkable successes. I, like most U.S. physicians, know very little about herbal therapy, but I have had too many patients reporting benefits from them to discount their value. Preparations such as Ginseng, Dong Quai, Black Cohosh, Evening Prim-

rose, Borage Seed Oil, and Simplex F are all available at health food stores packaged individually or in herbal and vitamin formulations such as Nature's Way Product "Change-O-Life."

I can't imagine them being harmful, but users of these natural preparations must keep in mind that many of them do have estrogenic activity, and merely substituting an estrogen herb for a prescription estrogen doesn't make it necessarily safer. Estrogen is estrogen, regardless of the source. If you are apprehensive about HRT, you should also be concerned about estrogenic herbs and foods.

FOODS

Soya flour and linseed (also called flaxseed) are foods eaten in large quantities in some parts of the world. They are said to increase estrogen levels in postmenopausal women, according to Marilyn Shannon in her book *Fertility, Cycles and Nutrition* (Cincinnati: Couple to Couple, 1990). She recommends two ounces of soya flour or one ounce of linseed daily.

RELAXATION TECHNIQUES AND ACUPUNCTURE

Modern research has only limited experience with relaxation techniques and acupuncture for reducing the intensity and frequency of hot flashes. But again, many are helped by them, so why not?

These are things that you might consider to relieve the annoying short-term symptoms of menopause and still avoid hormone therapy.

What about the long-term consequences of estrogen deficiency? There are three major ones—osteoporosis, cardiovascular disease, and chronic vaginal dryness. In each case, there are less effective nonhormonal methods of prevention, and in each circumstance the seriousness of the problem might cause you to reconsider the use of hormones.

1. Osteoporosis: Get a bone density test to determine the status of your bone mass. If low or if you have a significant family history of osteoporosis or other risk factors (see chapter 6, Estrogen and Osteoporosis), you and your doctor together might reconsider the use of estrogen, perhaps in very low doses along with calcium and vitamin D.

   If, on the other hand, your bones are healthy, keep up on your calcium intake (1500 mg/day) along with vitamin D 400

I.U./day and maintain a good exercise program. These cannot do what estrogen in the usual preventive dose schedule does to forestall osteoporosis, but it is a good second line of defense.

Finally, repeat your bone density test every so often to be sure you are not losing the bone battle.

2. Cardiovascular disease: Consider your family's cardiovascular history. Find out about your own cholesterol profile. If you are at low risk for cardiovascular disease, then estrogens probably aren't necessary.

But continue to be vigilant in maintaining cardiovascular health by staying trim, eating a low-fat diet, and staying faithful to aerobic exercises.

On the other hand, if your cholesterols and family history place you in a high-risk category, at least be willing to discuss the possible use of estrogen for its known ability to reduce the risk.

3. Vaginal dryness: Over-the-counter lubricants, like Replens or Comfort, can be tried first. Most find them a little disappointing. Consider using estrogen vaginal cream twice a week. During the first four months your bloodstream will see signifi-

cant levels of absorbed estrogen, but after that, when the vagina regains its softness and surface integrity, it becomes more of a barrier to estrogen absorption.

I expect to see in the future weakly concentrated vaginal estrogen creams that will work locally with little absorption into the system. There is one new product like this available in Europe right now, but it is not yet available in the U.S.

❦

NINE

Breast Cancer Patients and Estrogen

TOPPLING OF A MEDICAL ICON

An estrogen boycott was foisted upon breast cancer victims many years ago. It was thought that estrogen usage was "like pouring gasoline on a fire." Today that concept is being challenged by those who are revisiting the old data and looking at the new. Their findings strongly suggest that the use of estrogen may not be harmful to breast cancer; in fact, it may even prevent recurrences, and I believe one day soon it will be removed from the list of absolute contraindications.

In the last few years some very courageous investigators have been questioning the medical axiom—Once breast cancer, never estrogens. Even the FDA questioned it when its advisory committee recently (1993) decided that it was time to permit research investigations offering estrogen to women, who have had breast cancer. The FDA reasoned that protection against osteoporosis and cardiovascular disease was so vital for women, and since no one really knew whether estrogen truly did represent a risk to the women who have had breast cancer, that further investigation was deemed appropriate.

Challenging this long-entrenched taboo probably started anecdotally when some doctors would quietly prescribe estrogen to desperately symptomatic breast-cancer patients. In fact, a fairly recent poll taken by obstetricians and gynecologists across the country found that 61 percent admitted writing estrogen prescriptions for their patients (either in the form of vaginal cream or low-dose oral estrogen).[1] It appeared that everybody's experience was the same—that estrogen replacement did not have any untoward effects on the tumor.

The next step was to review the medical experiences of those patients who were found to have breast cancer at times of high estrogen exposure—such as pregnancy. In this situation it had always been thought that the outlook was dismal because of the adverse effect of high levels of circulating estrogen. At one time pregnancies were even terminated to protect the expectant mother. Later, however, it was discovered that terminating a pregnancy, either by abortion or by delivering the baby early, did *not* improve the patient's cancer outcome. Science learned the hard way! The reason why patients appeared to do so poorly when their cancers were discovered during pregnancy was *because they were young, not because they were pregnant!* This was validated when it was learned that *young* women who were *not* pregnant faced a survival rate that was virtually the same. Moreover, breast cancer patients who later became pregnant did just as well as those who didn't.[2]

These findings and others caused investigators like Dr. Philip J. DiSaia, professor and director of gynecological oncology at the University of California, Irvine, to seriously reassess the whole subject of estrogen prohibition. Dr. DiSaia now states, "There is no substantial evidence of an association between high levels of estrogen either of endogenous or exogenous source and the development of breast cancer, or that estrogen results in the exacerbation of existing breast cancer."[3]

Dr. Philip J. Maguire has written one of the

best overall scientific summaries indicating where we now stand in respect to the use of estrogen in breast cancer patients. He concludes,

> *Estrogen replacement therapy has been shown to improve bone structure and reduce cardiovascular disease as well as suppressing many of the well-known and disagreeable symptoms of menopause. Since 1942, numerous studies have attempted to relate its use to breast cancer. With the possible exception of a strong positive family history of breast cancer, there is no consistent evidence that estrogen therapy adversely affects the breast. In view of the unquestionable value in improving the quality of life, it seems unfair to withhold this therapy from patients with breast cancer.*[4]

Adding to the mounting data are thirty cases of breast cancer treated with HRT by Dr. John Studd of London, England, and ninety cases from Australia treated by Dr. J. A. Eden in which there were no deaths in any of the 120 patients given estrogen and a significantly lower recurrence rate in users compared to nonusers (25 percent versus 6 percent).[5]

A thorough up-to-date summary on this subject is written by Dr. Leon Speroff in *Contemporary Ob/Gyn* (July 1993). This issue may still be available from *Contemporary Ob/Gyn,* Montvale, NJ 07645-1742 for ten dollars a copy.

WHAT DOES ALL THIS MEAN?

What does this mean to you if you have had breast cancer? It means that you now have the opportunity, if you choose, to find relief from intolerable menopausal symptoms with estrogen therapy; furthermore, it is available as part of your preventive health program. But you must remember that it is *not yet* FDA approved, and most of us in the profession agree that many more investigational studies are needed before all of us can feel totally comfortable in doing something that has for so long been medically forbidden. Taking estrogen could still present a risk to the patient who has been treated for breast cancer. This risk could be slight. It could be serious. On the other hand, there could be no risk at all and may even be beneficial.

The bottom line is, once again, women must decide with too little information. It means weighing unknown benefits against unknown risks. It must be your choice but, again, a choice you should make jointly with your doctor, the one who knows your history, since every case has to be individualized. But don't be surprised if he or she asks for a signed informed consent. I still do but only for medical legal protection. I remain particularly concerned about giving estrogen to a patient with very recent breast cancer, especially one that involved lymph nodes or positive estrogen receptors at the time of surgery. I still am uneasy about prescribing estrogen for women who have always been considered at high risk for getting breast cancer in the first place—a positive family history, early onset of periods, late menopause, late onset of first pregnancy, non-breast-feeders, the obese, and those hooked on high-fat diets. Again, it depends on how serious one's symptoms and medical needs are and whether estrogen alternatives have failed (see chapter 8, Alternatives to Estrogen).

But I must say the data thus far presented is both compelling and convincing, especially when one weighs a 50 percent reduction in heart disease against what appears to be a low reoccurrence risk to breast cancer survivors using estrogen.

If one does decide in favor of taking estrogen, many authorities would advise taking progestin along with it.[6] The reason, according to

Dr. Fred Naftolin, chairman of Yale's Department of Obstetrics and Gynecology, is that progestin reduces the number of estrogen receptors.

TAMOXIFEN

Today many breast cancer patients, especially younger ones, are receiving a drug called tamoxifen (trade name Nolvadex) to prevent the recurrence of their cancers. It was originally designed for but never used to induce ovulation in infertility patients. It is a rather unusual drug in that it has both estrogenic and anti-estrogenic properties. However, its most significant feature is its ability to block estrogen receptors, preventing any circulating estrogen from "locking in."

Like estrogen, it appears to reduce the risk of cardiovascular disease and osteoporosis. That's good news. But, unfortunately it also increases the activity of the endometrial lining of the uterus. That's bad news. Thus all patients taking tamoxifen and who have a uterus need to be carefully monitored annually with pelvic ultrasound, endometrial biopsy, or both to rule out developing endometrial hyperplasia, the precursor to uterine cancer.

Tamoxifen's anti-estrogenic properties can

be quite disturbing, for it often causes hot flashes and vaginal dryness. Dr. DiSaia of the University of California School of Medicine at Irvine, when confronted with patients with these distressing symptoms will prescribe estrogen and progestin along with the tamoxifen. In contrast, Dr. Speroff of the University of Oregon School of Medicine prefers not to, at least until more studies have attested to their safety.

The management of breast cancer has changed dramatically in the past few years. Radical, disfiguring operations have in most cases given way to limited surgery and radiation. Postoperative chemotherapy now often includes tamoxifen, a drug similar in action to estrogen. And finally, estrogen for menopausal side effects is no longer being empirically prohibited. All of this has placed a much bigger decision-making role on the shoulders of every person who is diagnosed as having breast cancer. But, as the Bible says, "In the multitude of counsellors there is safety." So get it! This is one time in a woman's life when she should discuss the issue with those she trusts and those she knows have practical experience in the field.

One final point about tamoxifen. There is

currently an ongoing trial sponsored by the National Cancer Institute to determine if it is effective in preventing women who have a strong family history of breast cancer from developing the disease.

TEN

❧

Sexuality in Mid-Life

WE know that a woman's sexuality is more than just thinking about sex or having sex. It includes how she perceives herself as a sexual being and what she believes others think about her sexually. It involves her senses and so involves sensual reactions to things not necessarily sexual—the pleasurable feeling of silk sliding over her skin, a warm tropic breeze caressing her body, or the earthy, masculine scent of a man's cologne.

A woman's sexuality is a lifelong learning process and not just some serendipitous adulthood discovery. It embraces her thoughts, her attitudes, her perceptions, her reactions, as well as her physical responses. It is all these things woven together like a fine tapestry—unique—the individual expression of her femininity and sexual makeup.

Because a woman's sexuality is so much more than mere physical sensation and sexual performance, a woman's sexual experience in her mid-life years can be significant and satisfying. In fact, I believe that many mid-life women can enjoy greater sexual fulfillment than they did earlier in their lives.

THE EFFECTS OF AGING ON SEXUALITY

In most women, menopause brings on fears of aging and, along with that, fears of losing sexual desire and attractiveness. But many of these fears are myths.

Admittedly, it can get downright confusing. Do mid-life and menopause diminish a woman's sexual drive or not? Fortunately, it is now possible to separate myth from truth, thanks to the incomparable work of two respected sex researchers, William H. Masters and Virginia E. Johnson.

Together they have compiled and written the most accurate and definitive data on the effect of age on human sexuality. Their work in the area of sex research has become medicine's "gold standard" to which most all sexual re-searchers refer. Their article "Sex and the Aging Process" is, in my opinion, the finest treatise ever written on this subject.[1] (Admit-tedly the age-related changes they describe really begin at the end of mid-life—the middle and late fifties. At first glance this would seem to make the following material less applicable to women in early mid-life. But, in fact, the information is just as important for them as it is for older individuals because it permits them to prepare for and to be ready for these inevitable anatomic and physiologic changes when they do come. It is this readiness and accommoda-tion that is the very key to maintaining a healthy sexual relationship during later years.)

Sexual Capacity

One of the first great myths that the work of Masters and Johnson refutes is that age causes a loss of sexual capacity. That is simply not true. Yes, there are changes that take place as we get older that may influence our sexual interest and performance (which we will discuss shortly), but the capacity to enjoy sex to the maximum is never lost—unless, of course, we let it! In fact, it should get better with age. The old adage "We're not getting older, we're just getting better" can be a reality for every couple regardless of age—if they wish. I add "if they wish" because there is a certain amount of personal responsibility and action we have to take so as not to allow age-related changes to dampen the enjoyment of sex.

A woman's capacity to have and enjoy sex does not change as she gets older. But the anatomical "parts" with which she has sex do change. Masters and Johnson in their clinical investigation found objective evidence of both anatomical and physiological alterations that can influence a woman's sexual response. The nipples of older women, for example, tend to be less erect and enlarged during the excitement phase of the sexual act itself. Also the clitoris, labia minora, and labia majora don't show as much engorgement as in their younger counterparts. Muscular contractions of the vagina, so prominent during younger years, become weaker. The amount of vaginal lubrication (the female counterpart of the male's erective process) decreases and is slower to develop. The vaginal walls become thinner and less expansive and less able to lengthen and increase their diameter in response to sexual stimulation. This can lend itself to small damaging cuts or fissures in the vaginal wall with intercourse.

Masters and Johnson write, "To be fore-warned . . . is to be forearmed." In other words, if you know these changes are coming and if you are prepared for them, there is no need to panic when they actually start to happen. As we shall see, estrogen is one of the big remedies for these physiological changes, but even in cases where estrogen cannot be prescribed, a woman and her mate can adapt, together. In either case, there is no reason why the sexual experience can't be better than ever.

Sexual Interest

It has been said that there is a natural decrease in sexual interest (libido) that comes with age. Is this myth or fact? Most investigators have to conclude that overall it is fact, but there are many exceptions.

Libido refers to our sexual urge or inter-est—our sex drive. When it is low, it means there is little or no interest in participating in the act. Sex is possible; it's just not desired. A diminished libido expresses itself in different ways. It is evident when a person becomes resistant to sexual arousal. It can be mani-fested by a reluctance to initiate or participate in sexual contact. Or it may be seen as being "turned off" by another's sexual advances.

The person who has lost his or her libido is just plain not interested in sex!

The intensity of a woman's sex interest peaks in her late thirties and early forties and continues at a high level for many years, well into her seventies for most. This is because male hormones called androgens (a group of hormones that include testosterone) continue to be manufactured by a woman's ovaries and adrenal glands long after the menopause. Androgens are the ones responsible for the sex drive in both men and women.

A man's sexual desire, on the other hand, peaks at age eighteen, and then after age thirty-five or so it gradually tapers. So when the wife's sex drive is still rising, her husband's is on the decline. This asynchronism doesn't make for a happy situation unless couples recognize their biological differences, discuss them openly together, and make the necessary adjustments.

Masters and Johnson as well as others have studied the effect age has on sexual interest. They admit that there is a detectable decrease in sexual desire, and it is more evident in men than women. They remind us that at sixty-five to seventy years of age we do not have the sexual appetite we did at age twenty-five. But neither do we have the physical energy or stamina in general that we had then.

Though age is a reason for a decline in one's libido, perhaps the most common reason has to do with relationships. Where there is conflict and strife between two parties, whether expressed or not expressed, where there is resentment or lack of trust, ultimately there is going to be a loss of sexual interest. Sex is a barometer of what is going on in all the other rooms in the home besides the bedroom.

Stress is another common cause of a sagging libido. The reason sexual disorders are so common today is that we live in such stressful times. The rat race takes over our mind and shoves "sex" way to the back where it must struggle to regain our attention. Illness, depression, financial difficulties, drugs—including alcohol—and fear of pregnancy are common stress causes of a diminished interest in sex. Another important reason for loss of libido has to do with how we perceive ourselves physically.

James Dobson, in his outstanding book *What Wives Wish Their Husbands Knew about Women*, reminds us of the importance of attitude and self-image on a woman's sexuality: "If a woman sees herself as old and unattractive, she might lose interest in sex for reasons only secondary to her age."[2] In fact, the sex drive is probably the collective result of all these things. The effects of aging on sexual appetite may be over-estimated.

Sexual Climax

One rather common old wives' tale is that women have fewer orgasms as they grow older. Masters and Johnson's data expose this for what it is—a total fabrication and a myth that can now be banished forever.

Their findings do confirm that older women were slower to achieve orgasm, and their orgasms were less intense than during their earlier years. But there was no change in either their capacity to have orgasms or their subjective appreciation for the experience.

Some older women do experience pain with orgasm. This is explained by the appearance of a dysfunction in the usually well-coordinated contractions of the uterine musculature that are companion to a woman's climax. This, like most of the sex-hindering vaginal changes, is improved or avoided altogether with estrogen replacement.

Male sexual climax seems to decline more

with age than does a woman's. Erections take longer to achieve and are less firm than during peak years of sexual prowess. Older men seem to require more genital touching for stimulation, as their visual "turn-on" mechanisms to "real or presumed sexual opportunity," so prominent in younger years, tend to falter. Masters and Johnson note that a man in his later years tends to have a "decrease in expulsive pressure and a reduction in the volume of the seminal fluid expelled during his ejaculatory experience." One distressing event for men is the occasional failure to ejaculate. This may take place as often as one out of three or four times men have intercourse and is often associated with a resumption of sex after long periods of abstinence for whatever reason.

Scientific research then shows that the capacity of women to enjoy sex and to consummate it with orgasm is something that does not change with age. On the other hand, there is a natural age-related alteration of the sex organs—and these "equipment" changes will have an impact on the ability to be sexually aroused. Knowing all this should help us to adjust to these changes and not to panic when these alterations actually do come about.

MAKING THE BEST OF WHAT YOU HAVE

Most elderly couples have to give up their sexual activity eventually because of the infirmities of advanced age. But some couples do a better job than others of extending the pleasures of sex. This is well illustrated by one patient of mine.

Lucille is seventy-nine years old. She first came to my office for a "routine" examination. Her husband was waiting with her in the exam room as I entered. They had been married fifty-three years and were still very much in love.

It had been some time since her last pelvic exam, and she had run out of her estrogen pills, which had been prescribed by another doctor. So she had not taken any for several months. When they came to my office that day, I asked her husband if he would like to stay while I examined her. He accepted the invitation.

As I examined her, I could see evidence of estrogen deficiency that had affected the vagina, leaving it pale and dry. From his chair nearby I heard him nervously clear his throat and then ask, "Say, Doc, would you mind sort of checking out the vagina?"

As he said it, Lucille giggled.

With an impish grin he said, "It seems . . . well, it seems a little dryer than it used to be. We still like to . . . you know . . . fool around some, if you know what I mean."

It seems to me that every elderly couple, like this delightful pair, ought to give up sex with great reluctance—make it a last resort!

This couple maintained an active sex life for many years. When they saw that it was being compromised, they sought help. This is a good lesson for all couples as they grow older together—never willingly give up. Never accept the lie that sexual enjoyment comes to a screeching halt as you get older. If something begins to interfere with the pleasure it brings, seek help. If it is something that is not correctable, perhaps something such as ailing health or whatever, then accept it, be open about it with each other, and adapt to it. Live contentedly with what you have and make the most of it! Caress each other with words of loving-kindness and demonstrate physical appreciation in other ways.

SEX AND MENOPAUSE
Just as there are many myths about age and human sexuality, there are just as many floating around about menopause and sexuality. One

myth that needs to be put to rest once and for all is that menopause is the beginning of a sexless life. The arrival of menopause need never dampen a woman's sexual experience, but unfortunately too often it does.

A woman knows that menopause spells the loss of reproductive capacity. Even though she may know better, she still tends to equate loss of her reproductive potential to loss of "womanhood."

One thing that perpetuates this misconception is that menopause is a convenient scapegoat. Many things push sex out of one's mind during the mid-life years. They shouldn't, but they do. Problems with children, dissatisfaction with the marriage, extramarital affairs, problems at work, finances, failure to realize dreams and goals of life—whatever it is that captures one's preoccupation will usually sap one's sexual interest. Rather than admit what the real culprit is, many a woman blames her disappointing sexual experience on menopause. "Menopause has literally destroyed my sex life!" we sometimes hear. In reality it is the stress events in a woman's daily routine that are "destroying" her sex life.

A man may contribute to this particular myth, too. Perhaps seeing or fearing a faltering of his own sexual interest or sexual performance, he will often use the old "my wife's going through menopause" excuse. But it is nothing more than an avoidance mechanism that allows him to sidestep what is actually taking place in his own life (see chapter 12, Making the Most of Mid-Life).

The truth is that menopause itself does not suspend sexual desire or capacity. Menopause (treated or not treated, depending on the need), can be a delightful extension of a woman's femininity and sexual being. In fact, many menopausal women experience an increase in their libido during this time of life. They are usually women who, during their reproductive years, regularly experienced a rising interest in sex just before and during their menstrual period—a time of lowered estrogen, just like menopause.

Many menopause patients we see in our office do admit to decreased sexual interest. But having worked extensively with menopausal women for the past few years, I'm convinced that diminished libido is not very much estrogen related. When you give back to a woman her estrogen in the form of hormone replacement, it doesn't improve her sexual interest all that much. Some note an improvement, others don't. And I believe the "improvement" is often attributable to the overall sense of well-being that women experience when they take estrogen—generally speaking when we feel better, sex feels better.

Another "apparent" association of decreased sexual desire and menopause is also questionable. If a woman suffers from severe vaginal dryness and intercourse causes her to hurt for hours or even days afterward, you can be sure there is little inducement for her to want sex! As stated earlier, this is correctable and need not be an ongoing menopausal condition.

AVOIDING SEXUAL PROBLEMS IN MID-LIFE

The best way to make the most of your sexuality in mid-life is, of course, to work at having a good marriage. This is sometimes easier said than done—but it still needs to be said! It is on this basis—a relationship with a mutual interest in satisfying the other partner—that the mid-life woman and her husband can build a more satisfying sexual relationship in the following ways:

Proper Knowledge

So much about sex is enshrouded in secrecy, but for those raised in strict, provincial homes it can be even more of a mystery. Couples will struggle if they are sharing the bedroom with a third party—ignorance. Fortunately we are seeing this begin to change. Marital counselors now focus on this very important subject more than ever before.

The mid-life woman must realize that, as her marriage evolves as the years go by, the importance and need for knowledge about sexual matters does not stop. For example, lack of information about the inexorable changes in the sex organs that come with age can devastate a marriage. Masters and Johnson write,

For the uninformed female partner, lack of knowledge of possible alteration in her aging partner's sexual response patterning also poses potentially serious psychosexual problems. When any physiologic changes in sexual response become obvious in her male partner [meaning diminished interest in sex, an inability to have or sustain an erection, or failure to consummate the sexual experience with ejaculation], her initial reaction may be to question her own sexuality. His obviously slowed erective response may be interpreted as loss of interest in her . . . that he doesn't need her, or she may fear that he has identi-

fied some other sexual interest. These questions do arise and, with the usual lack of communicative facility about sexual matters that is commonplace in American families, the questions may be left unanswered or on a presumptive basis answered incorrectly to the detriment of the particular relationship.[3]

Smart couples will learn what is happening to their bodies, prepare themselves for changes, and communicate with each other when such changes make their appearance. In that way, it is less likely for spouses to be disappointed in themselves or their mates—no high expectations, no disappointments, no anxieties.

Good Communication

A couple needs to express comfortably their own needs and desires to each other. At first it may seem awkward, but with time it can become natural.

Every marital relationship should include an openness that permits each partner to indicate when sex is not on his or her mind without hurting the other's feelings or causing the other to feel rejected. Likewise, there are times when one party of the marriage just plain needs sex. Tension builds, and the emotional release that sex offers is needed. All one should really have to do is say so! Maybe the spouse isn't in the mood. But most of the time he or she would want to know; many times he or she would be very much willing. But the "needy" party should not forget to acknowledge his or her love and appreciation toward that one who was willing!

Often a mid-life woman remains sexually unfulfilled, yet says nothing to her husband for fear of hurting his feelings or ego. She is not being fair to him by withholding this information. In a way it's deceitful. She must tell him. How can the sexual aspect of the marriage improve if one member is not even aware there is a problem?

Some women have inhibitions about communicating more specific sexual feelings and desires, perhaps thinking, *If I show him what makes me feel good, he'll think I do it to myself when I'm alone.* So, nothing is said, and the naive, noncommunicating couple remains in a sexual rut, both just enduring, both left short of fulfillment.

Let's face it—sex is fun, pleasurable, and relaxing. It shouldn't be something to be embarrassed about. In marriage it needs to be a topic of ongoing conversation. In a mid-life marriage, even more communication is necessary.

Creativity

With any relationship, the sexual relationship is something we have to work at. Wise couples will not allow their sexual intercourse to become humdrum, conventional, and void of creativity. So when either husband or wife wishes to try something sexually different, then he or she should just say so. It's that simple. In the marriage bed, creativity should reign unless it causes pain, embarrassment, or disrespect.

Passion

A woman needs more than routine mechanics in the lovemaking process. It takes time and passion to arouse her sensuality so she can respond to her mate. When there is routine— the same time, place, method—it leads to boredom and then lack of enthusiasm. Passion is the very essence that keeps us interested in our sexual relationships.

We notice one negative pattern in many mid-life marriages. Kissing has become perfunctory. A kiss between a mid-life wife and husband is often just a routine peck on the lips. Whatever happened to the passionate kiss?

Distractions

Fatigue, stress, job worries, finances, depression, fear of getting pregnant—anything that holds our minds captive when we're in bed—are the thieves of sexual pleasure and fulfillment. As one patient shared with Mary, "Right in the middle of having sex, my mind wanders to other thoughts. You know, it's crazy! But I find myself thinking about what I need to pick up at the cleaners, what I'm going to wear tomorrow night, did I put the cat out? It really is crazy! I just can't seem to concentrate. I love my husband, and I enjoy sex, but my mind just won't turn off."

The solution is to share these distractions. "Honey, I'm stressed out. I'm sorry, but sex seems to be the last thing on my mind right now. But if it's on yours, then tell me." This breaks the ice. The destructive mind-reading game— *Are we or aren't we going to have sex?*—stops.

A woman should try to be sensitive to her husband's sexual machinery. When it's cranked up, it's difficult to turn off. So the smart wife will not stir her mate sexually if there will be no fait accompli. For example, if a woman is in her period and thinking, *Tonight is not the night,* she really should let her husband know. If she feels uncomfortable verbalizing it, then she can do it in a more subtle way, perhaps by placing a tampon or sanitary pad in a discreet location in the bathroom, where her husband won't miss seeing it. This averts any possible frustration or embarrassment on his part and avoids "injury" to a delicate ego (common to all men).

Personal Hygiene

Another factor that precludes sexual problems is good personal hygiene. A woman owes it to her partner to keep herself clean, well-groomed, looking nice, and smelling good. If she becomes careless and allows herself to become slothful in her body care and appearance, she really does jeopardize her marriage. Not only does this·kind of irresponsibility turn a spouse off, it also creates a potential stumbling block. If a wife allows herself to become a slob, she subjects her spouse to the sexual temptations out there in the nonslob world! The same applies to her spouse, too!

Good Health

Obviously, if a woman has an illness, acutely or chronically, it will affect her ability to have and enjoy sex. More important, if she is just frequently under the weather or fatigued or always just coming down with the latest cold or flu, she sabotages the sexual experience. This points out the need to take care of one's body. It is one more call for the need to practice good preventive medicine.

Mutually Agreed-Upon Abstinence with Age

Age can bring with it chronic illnesses, heart trouble, arthritis, diabetes, etc. Too often, however, these become excuses to avoid sex. This is wrong because sex can have a tranquil, relaxing effect on the body and be just what the doctor ordered. Some heart-attack victims are frightened that sex may cause another one. But cardiologists offer a good practical test. If a person can climb two flights of stairs without discomfort, his heart is not going to be unduly stressed by sex. Some medical illnesses that come with age may demand abstinence. When this happens, openness and frankness with each other are critically important. As couples become elderly, many are forced to give up sex altogether. It just needs to be replaced with a different kind of sexual intimacy—good sex substitutes called hugging, kissing, stroking, and of course verbal expressions of appreciation of one another.

TREATMENT OF SEXUAL DISORDERS

There are a variety of male and female sexual disorders that physicians must treat. Inability to achieve orgasm, painful intercourse, impotency, and premature ejaculation are just a few.

Many of them simply mirror a turbulent, dysfunctional marriage, while others originate during earlier years of life.

The key to correcting sexual disorders is to figure out the root cause as quickly as possible. It is best not to get bogged down with the "symptom." For example, a patient's chief complaint may be painful intercourse. That is the symptom. But the "disease" may be the fact that the woman was sexually abused as a child. Before the coital problem can be resolved, a woman must first deal with the guilt that so often accompanies this kind of childhood trauma. This usually requires long-term therapy by someone skilled and trained in sexual abuse. The sexually abused victim has to be taken back to the time of the dreadful ordeal to permit her to see once and for all that she was merely the innocent victim and what took place was not her fault.

Once we address and resolve the foundational issues, the sexual problem—the symptom—can be treated.

Failure to Achieve Orgasm

One of the most common sexual disorders in women is the inability to reach orgasm. It can leave its sufferer feeling frustration, disappointment, and maybe even guilt.

186

Orgasm is something a woman reaches at the peak of her sexual response. It brings intense pleasure and a sense of achievement. This satisfying feeling is accompanied by involuntary, rhythmic contractions in the muscles surrounding the vagina, uterus, and pelvic floor and leaves her feeling sensual, relaxed, and content. This pinnacle of delight is all she needs at that moment, and, in fact, further touching of the genital area can be very uncomfortable for her for a short period of time.

The reasons for a failure to reach orgasm are many, but high on the list is the simple lack of knowledge by either partner—but most often the husband. Many men view themselves as "sex encyclopedias," when more often than not they're still in the "sex primer" stage. Usually it's an ego-booster for a man to think he knows how to satisfy a woman sexually; often he's fooling himself with the smattering of knowledge he has picked up from a variety of unqualified sources.

The most common mistake a man can make is failing to recognize that his wife's number one sex organ (just like his) is her mind, not her clitoris, which, of course, all men have heard about. The role of the clitoris in sexual satisfaction is paramount, but foreplay "quickies" won't always do the job. In fact, quality foreplay should begin in the kitchen. As one patient confided to me about her disappointing marital relationship with her "foreplay-stingy" husband, "I need to be treated nice standing up before I lie down!"

Men are visual. Show them a nude female body, and they're turned on instantly. Signals travel from their brains to the penis in less than nanoseconds. Women, on the other hand, need to feel secure and need to feel love through cuddling, touching, and vocal reassurances. That takes time. As speaker and writer Gary Smalley quips, "Men are like microwaves . . . but women are more like Crock-Pots." (To that I would add that every husband who ignores this fact of life will wind up in hot soup!)

Another reason some women remain non-orgasmic is a misunderstanding about the physiology of orgasm itself. Only a minority of women achieve orgasm with "no-hands" intercourse. Most women require continual, gentle, often prolonged manual stimulation of the clitoris, of their breasts, and of other sensual areas of their bodies before and during intercourse. They may even need to be involved in the process themselves.

For many young couples it may take months

or even years for the woman to experience orgasm. For them, time alone is all that is necessary. But orgasm is always going to elude a small percentage of women despite good knowledge, good techniques, and good counseling. Still it should never be considered a failure where warmth and tenderness prevail. Sexual intercourse does not always have to include orgasm to be satisfying for a woman.

I have one patient who confided to me in frustration that her husband in all the years of their marriage never once offered her any foreplay. It broke her heart. At one point it got so bad she even begged him. He only let out a macho grunt, said nothing, and when he had satisfied himself, rolled over and went to sleep.

I can't imagine anyone being this cruel and selfish, but it's done all the time by men who don't understand how much this kind of closeness means to a woman. This husband probably views himself as a real man, but in reality he is only a selfish child.

Of all the things that will most help a woman to reach a satisfying climax is knowing that her husband loves her, respects her, and is committed to please her and care for her. You see, it's the mind again. When a woman feels this kind of confidence and security in her marital relationship, she maximizes her experience of the joy of sexual freedom, excitement, and fulfillment.

Diminished Libido

Diminished interest in sex is one of the most common sexual complaints of a mid-life woman. Many menopausal women are disappointed when they see no improvement when they go on estrogen therapy. But, in fact, estrogen's most important contribution to increasing sexual interest is to keep the vagina well lubricated, thus avoiding painful intercourse. When estrogen improves a failing libido, it is probably secondary to an improved self-esteem.

As previously mentioned, a diminished interest in sex can be related to age, stress, or eroded relationships. Recently there has been a revival in the use of testosterone in an attempt to treat this problem regardless of the cause. It has been shown that testosterone does significantly and favorably influence a woman's libido. However, many women are hesitant to consider taking a male hormone like testosterone. But they shouldn't. Actually malelike hormones, called androgens (the most potent being testosterone), are common to both men and women. In fact, the production of androgens by the adrenal gland is equal in both sexes. The ovaries are the chief source of testosterone in women both before and after menopause.

It is better to think of testosterone not just as a male sex hormone but rather an "in-between" compound on its way to forming female hormones. For example, the ovaries convert cholesterol, the basic building block, to progesterone, then to testosterone, then to estrogen. So testosterone is the immediate precursor to estrogen. Indeed, at any given time in the bloodstream of the premenopausal woman will be found some progesterone, some testosterone, and some estrogen, in varying amounts.

Many people believe testosterone is the opposite of estrogen. It is not. In small dosage it even has weak estrogen activity.

One study concluded that testosterone therapy is suitable for women with loss of sexual drive and libido especially when combined with estrogen.[4] Other studies have shown only an increase in sexual fantasies but not frequency of sex or sexual satisfaction.

In our experience, testosterone enhances libido and general sexual satisfaction in about half of the women who receive it. The injections seem to work better. Not surprising, those who respond are very pleased with its effect and stay on testosterone supplement for a long period of time.

Testosterone is available for oral use, by pellet implants beneath the skin, or intramuscular injections.

What about side effects of testosterone? Frankly, there are very few seen in the doses we normally use. Mild facial hair, oily skin, and acne are seen in less than 5 percent of women when the total monthly dosages are kept under 75 mg. That increases to 15 percent when the monthly dosage is doubled to 150 mg. Side effects are always reversible when testosterone is stopped.

Past concerns that testosterone might have an adverse effect on cholesterol have been eliminated by more recent clinical findings that show that estrogen-testosterone therapy has an insignificant effect on the cholesterol profile.[5]

More recently a concern has been raised about testosterone's effect on the liver. However, the potential for testosterone to cause liver damage appears to be only in very high dosages, far greater than that being used for androgen replacement today.

Painful Intercourse
There are many medical reasons for painful intercourse (dyspareunia)—infection, ovarian

cysts, displaced uterus, pelvic congestion, endometriosis, adhesions, etc. But statistically the most common cause of painful intercourse is insufficient lubrication, usually from inadequate foreplay—in other words the "Crock-Pot" has not been given sufficient time to warm up.

Painful intercourse can also be the result of vaginal dryness and irritation from estrogen deficiency (see chapter 3, Understanding Menopause). When the vagina becomes dry from insufficient estrogen, we call it atrophic vaginitis. In this condition the lining of the vaginal wall becomes thin (as much as one-fifth the thickness of the premenopausal vagina), rigid, and nonpliable.

There is only one cure for atrophic vaginitis, and that is estrogen. Estrogen will almost immediately restore a woman's ability to lubricate naturally. It achieves this by encouraging the cells of the vaginal wall to build up and become thicker. This thickening brings with it a rich network of blood vessels. This is important: Since there are no lubricating glands in the vaginal walls, all lubrication must be "sweated" into the vagina from encircling blood vessels. So it's simple mathematics. The more estrogen, the more blood vessels. The more blood vessels, the more lubrication.

Even with adequate estrogen and effective foreplay, however, lubricants do help improve intercourse at all ages. No nightstand or suitcase should be without a tube. I recommend using the water soluble lubricants rather than Vaseline because some women are sensitive to its petroleum base. Also, it is a little harder to remove than water soluble lubricants. Some women will even use a little estrogen cream placed just at the opening of the vagina to not only allow the penis to enter the vagina more comfortably but to also help disperse the estrogen into the vaginal wall with intercourse.

There is something else that encourages vaginal moistening. It probably comes under the category of "use it or lose it." Studies have shown that regular sexual activity maximizes the natural lubricating benefits of estrogen and prevents vaginal shrinkage that accompanies aging.

Finally, painful intercourse can also have a psychological basis, resulting in a condition known as "vaginismus." The muscles around the vagina become so tense that intercourse becomes virtually impossible. Attempts at vaginal penetration then cause more spasms of the muscles, more pain, and a vicious cycle becomes established. Women with vaginismus frequently are victims of childhood sexual abuse.

Impotence

Men also have sexual difficulty for many of the same reasons as women. Certainly one of the most disturbing is impotence, the inability to achieve and maintain an erection. It can be devastating for a married couple. Impotence can be caused by medical problems such as diabetes or arteriosclerosis. It can result from the use of certain medications, drugs, or alcohol. It also occurs after radical prostate surgery for cancer.

Most often, however, it is emotionally induced by depression, anxiety, or stress—either at home or at work. Most men at one time or another have experienced the problem of impotence. But when it becomes a chronic, recurring problem, then it requires professional help. Today there are good prostheses for men to mechanically induce an erection.

Premature Ejaculation

Premature ejaculation can be another distressing problem for a couple. Not only is it an embarrassment for the husband, it can also interfere with a wife's ability to achieve an orgasm. But premature ejaculation can actually be overcome, if not cured, through counseling and instruction in certain techniques and sexual exercises.

Dealing with Sexual Disorders

Most minor sexual disturbances resolve themselves with time and open communication. But there are some that don't. They need to be professionally diagnosed and treated.

Probably the first person a mid-life woman should talk to about a sexual disturbance is her gynecologist. An exam may uncover simple, easily correctable hormonal or anatomical problems.

If the problem is psychological and not physical, it needs to be tackled with the help of a counselor as quickly as possible. This is no time for procrastination. Counseling saves precious time by identifying and dealing with such root problems as fear, guilt, stress, extreme modesty, discordant marriages, physical abuse, verbal abuse, and emotional abuse.

Occasionally a sex therapist may have to be brought into the picture. When that becomes necessary, however, one must be careful to choose someone who is skilled, experienced, and reputable. There are many unqualified people who call themselves sex therapists but are not. A local county medical association or a university-affiliated medical center are often good sources to recommend competent sex therapists.

It is always wrong for the mid-life couple to "throw in the towel" if they begin to experience climactic disappointments. Both need to face the problem head on, courageously, aggressively—perhaps to the point of seeking professional help. But the most important admonition to mid-life couples is this: Gently reassure each other of your love and appreciation and learn to not expect so much from each other. In the mid-life marriage the husband and wife need each other and depend on each other. They should never forget that they are a team and will probably play on this same team for the rest of their lives.

For the woman facing menopause and mid-life, she should know that this phase of her life doesn't have to mean sexual decline. In fact, it can be one of the best times of her life, especially if her estrogen levels are maintained. She'll sleep better, have more energy, and enjoy a sense of well-being and self-confidence, which allows her to be sexually more at ease. And with no more fear of pregnancy or kids bursting into the bedroom at inopportune moments, mid-life can be a woman's sexual utopia.

What's more important, the mid-life woman should understand that her mind and body are capable of sexual pleasure for years to come. Sex will be what she makes it.

ELEVEN

❦

Maximizing Your Health in Mid-Life

WHEN was the last time you found yourself whistling when you felt sick?

Well, no one would deny that our attitude is dependent upon our health. When our health is good, it's easy to "feel" good. When our health is bad, it's not so easy.

If good attitude depends so much on our health, what can the mid-life woman do to maximize her chances of staying healthy?

ATTITUDES AND DISCIPLINE

Fortunately, there is much we can do. Unfortunately, it involves a lot of self-discipline, something that doesn't get easier as we get older.

Having to practice self-restraint isn't really

fair. Mid-life years should be a kind of reward time, a time to relax and not worry about things. I think this is particularly true of what we eat. Mid-lifers should be able to order a juicy steak whenever they wish or even some vanilla ice cream topped with caramel. But that's not the way it is.

Instead, mid-life finds most of us doing repair work on our bodies. We desperately try to restore the damage we did to ourselves during our younger years. Back then most of us took good health for granted—a big, but very human, mistake.

My father is now eighty-nine years old. He's a perfect human specimen—there's not an extra ounce of fat on him. A couple of years ago my brother Don and I took him on a hike back up into the Angeles Crest Forest. Dad whipped up those mountain trails like they were level paths, literally leaving us in the dust. Don and I were always stopping to catch our breath. We'd look at each other in disbelief. The only time Dad stopped was to let us catch up to him.

We both knew how a man more than thirty years our senior could do such a thing. As kids, every morning we could hear Dad downstairs doing his fifteen minutes of routine calisthenics and exercises. He never missed a day unless he was sick. He started this daily ritual when he was in high school, decades before exercise became vogue!

Dad had been disciplined in other areas of his life, long before health consciousness was the "in" thing. He instinctively chose fish and chicken over steak. He always ate in moderation and only fresh foods and vegetables. His only "vice" was an occasional dish of ice cream after dinner. I still remember how ritualistically he would scrape the surface of his ice cream—the tiniest of bites—savoring every delicious taste.

He never smoked or drank. His life has been the epitome of health and self-discipline. It is paying off in big dividends, which is why he can run up and down mountains with ease.

Mom, who died at seventy-six of a coronary, was not disciplined like Dad. She was raised on a farm and held to the prevailing philosophy—long before cholesterol became a household word—that there was nothing wrong with meat, potatoes, and gravy every night for dinner. For breakfast we ate eggs, pancakes, and cereal with cream on top of it. Her cakes and pies were her pride and joy. We were well fed and happy in our little home, not ever realizing the effect all this would have on our health later on.

So here we are in mid-life. Medical science has just informed us that the "good ol' American" diet wasn't so good after all. We all have to change our attitudes and habits if we expect to correct the cholesterolic wrongs of the past. For people like myself who find this kind of self-discipline difficult, practicing dietary preventive medicine is no piece of cake (so to speak!).

YOU ARE RESPONSIBLE

As today's woman, you should become actively involved in the decision making about your health care. To do this you will need to keep current on the latest medical facts. That is not always easy since medical "facts" keep changing. As valuable and useful as medical science is, it still frustrates. For example, researchers find coffee dangerous one year and safe the next. So you must just do the best you can, go after the most recent and authoritative sources possible, and use common sense. Keep in mind that true facts will pass the test of time.

In most doctors' offices you will find excellent pamphlets for patients on various health issues, prepared and distributed by the various medical specialties, in our case the American College of OB-GYN (ACOG). These pamphlets are concise, up-to-date, informative, and easily understood.

The most difficult decision to make is when your doctor recommends surgery. If and when that happens, make sure you understand why it is necessary and what the risks are. Ask to read something about the proposed surgery. You may even want to bring your husband, or another relative, back to the office with you on another visit to have the surgery explained to you both. And if you're still "on the fence," then don't hesitate to get a second opinion. You won't be hurting the doctor's feelings or ego (frankly, so what if it does?—it's your body!). Doctors are getting used to this since many insurance companies now require a second opinion before they will authorize major surgery.

REGULAR HEALTH EXAMS

Regular health exams cannot be emphasized enough. They are one of the best ways to assure both longevity and quality of life. Don't let "feeling lousy" be the only reason to see your doctor. One of the biggest mistakes a person can make is to assume that "if I feel OK, everything must be OK." That is simply not true.

The "routine" medical checkup is extremely

valuable; it's our first line of defense in the battle against disease, and it does save lives. It continues to amaze me as a practicing physician how often I find unsuspected problems, such as high blood pressure, abnormal heart rate, thyroid nodules, breast lumps, hernias, ovarian cysts—things that are correctable if found early before they get to a serious stage.

Many women rely on their gynecologist to do their routine annual exams. I don't believe that is enough. Usually our exams are more cursory and concentrate mostly on the breast and pelvic structures. Therefore, I encourage all of my patients over age forty to be examined regularly by their family practitioner or internist.

Find a physician who cares enough to allow *you* to make choices for yourself regarding your health care. Be assertive. Ask questions, and get answers in terms you can understand.

Document your regular health checkups. Keep a medical folder on yourself. At the front of the folder list the dates of your regular health exams, and then inside keep copies of your lab reports and notation of blood pressure and their dates. Your doctor will give you copies of your lab work if you just ask him.

When your blood pressure has been taken,

ask the doctor the values. Remember you are in charge of your health more than anyone else; if you aren't aware when something is wrong, how can you take steps to correct it? So be persistent. When the doctor tells you the blood pressure's actual value, write it down and later record it in your home medical folder. By keeping track of your test results, you can look for ominous, creeping trends in, for example, your cholesterol or blood pressure. A pressure of 142/90 might not be serious as a onetime recording, but if it represents a gradual upward climb over the past few years (something you will be able to spot by keeping records), it is a problem. In the past, physicians often attributed a slight elevation in blood pressure to the possible apprehension of actually going to a doctor—the so-called white-coat syndrome—and did not place much significance in it. Now, however, we look at it somewhat differently. It may be important to even treat this kind of "labile hypertension" because if it jumps up from the stress of going to the doctor's office, it may well be even higher with daily situational stress.

Note on your calendar when you are due for your next "ten-thousand-mile checkup." By the way, do you know who are the worst offenders of this principle of regular exams—the all-time procrastinators? Doctors themselves. I called my internist's office the other day to schedule my "yearly" exam, and the nurse laughed. "Yearly?" she said, poking fun. "Why, Dr. Wells, the last time you were in was five years ago. My, how time flies."

CARDIOVASCULAR DISEASE (CVD) PREVENTION

Cardiovascular disease (CVD) manifests itself in women around age sixty-five, about ten years later than men (see chapter 5, Estrogen and the Cardiovascular System). This increase corresponds to a woman's natural loss of estrogen through the process of menopause. So cardiovascular disease is not just a man's problem. In fact, one of every two women will die of either a heart attack or stroke. That makes it the number-one killer of women. An estimated five-hundred thousand lives a year are lost to this disease. What is amazing is that the majority are preventable!

There are hereditary influences over which we have no control. For example, the risk of CVD is higher in black women than in white women. Also, where mothers and fathers had CVD, the risk of heart attacks and strokes is higher in their offspring. But there are things a woman can do to prevent heart disease:

1. If You Smoke, Quit!

Smoking is a major risk factor for CVD, though lung cancer (with an incidence far less than CVD) receives more publicity as an argument against smoking. Lesser known facts are that smoking lowers estrogen blood levels and induces earlier menopause.

2. Eat Sensibly

We've all heard this plea before. And frankly, if you're like me, you're a little sick of hearing it. But it may be far more important to the maintenance of good health than previously thought.

Actually, little is known about diet. Often the ones who know the least are doctors. Most of us have received little or no training in it. We've learned about nutrition along with everyone else. We know, as you probably do, that proper nutrition means eating fresh fruits and vegetables instead of canned or frozen foods, and more fish and poultry than red meat.

Avoid quick junk foods loaded with calories and salt. Mary and I recently found out that this is not always easy when you have little ones. The more time we spend with our children and our granddaughter, we can see that in the interest of time and sanity a quick trip to McDonald's seems more appealing than listening to a little one cry while you're out in the kitchen preparing a "well-balanced meal." It's not always possible to avoid fast food, but still try. A handful of meals a month changed from fast food to healthful, balanced dinners can make a significant contribution to your health.

One final point about diet. When you are eating properly, you can reasonably expect higher energy levels and steadier emotions—a valuable side benefit.

3. Exercise Regularly

This accomplishes three health benefits and one relational benefit! First, it helps, though not as much as dieting, to reduce your weight. Second, it improves your cholesterol picture. Third, and probably its most important benefit, it cleans out the mental cobwebs. Just getting away briefly from strained, stressful circumstances is emotionally therapeutic for all of us. We recommend for the mid-life woman regular low-impact aerobics, brisk walking (two miles in thirty minutes) three times a week, tennis three times a week, or dancing, either "line" or ballroom (now gaining popularity because it's fun and is an excellent form of exercise).

Fourth, an additional bonus of walking is that it offers the much-needed opportunity for spouses to talk with each other. Every marriage needs uninterrupted time for communication.

4. Cut Back on High-Sodium Foods

The average American has a daily sodium intake of about 10 grams. It should be 2 or 3 grams. Salt is a major factor in the development of high blood pressure (hypertension). I know you're thinking, *But I love salt. I need it.* Try salt substitutes, herbal and lemon flavor. They are great.

5. Lose Weight If You Need To

Lose weight! That's another admonition portly folks like me are tired of hearing. (Mary is quite different from me in this area and has always kept within a few pounds of her ideal weight.) But staying trim is essential in our quest for good health. Do it for yourself! You can start by determining your ideal weight from a height and weight chart. Make that weight your goal. I always select from the "large-frame" column; the others seem depressingly unattainable. (Who determines "frame" sizes anyway?)

There is one discouraging fact about mid-life—it gets harder to lose weight than when you were younger. Another unfortunate observation I've noticed is that it is harder for women to lose weight than men. This probably has to do with metabolic differences in the two sexes, but I agree with you, it's simply not fair!

Some women can make the necessary adjustments on their own. Others do better on one of the many diet programs available in the community. Whatever works best for you, do it. You may need to shop around.

Weight loss alone will increase your longevity by reducing your blood pressure and by improving your cholesterol profile. And another bonus of weight loss is that it makes you more attractive to your mate and yourself!

6. Control Your Blood Pressure

This is something with which you must work closely with your doctor. If salt and calorie restriction is not working and your blood pressure is staying over 140/90 (some doctors would allow higher limits), then it may be time to begin a medication to keep it in the normal range (120–140/70–90). He will also most likely order as part of a basic hypertension workup an EKG or possibly a treadmill and blood tests.

Often just a mild diuretic taken daily is sufficient to keep it down. Today there are many safe and effective blood pressure–lowering drugs available that can be prescribed by your family physician or internist. Controlled hypertension should be a major goal in your quest for a healthy cardiovascular system. It gives you more active years of life.

7. Keep Your Cholesterol Under Control
As with your blood pressure, you will need to work closely with your doctor on this, too. Elevation in blood pressure and cholesterol are similar in that they both do their damage silently. For those who do not see their doctors for routine physical exams and blood tests, the first sign of hypertension could be a stroke, and the first evidence of high cholesterol a heart attack.

When you were young, your cholesterol levels were probably always in what we now consider the desirable range. But many women between forty-five and fifty-five experience a sharp increase in their total cholesterol levels to between 220 and 260 mg./dl. That is when your risk of heart attack begins to parallel men's. Your total cholesterol, however, should be kept less than 200, the low-density lipoprotein cholesterols (LDL-C) under 130 and your high-density lipoprotein-cholesterol (HDL-C) above 55. If your values do not fall within these preferred ranges, it's time for action. Even minor improvements in these values will bring about substantial reduction in your CVD risk. Use generous amounts of olive oil as a replacement for butter. It is probably one of the reasons our Mediterranean friends enjoy slim, healthy lives!

Experts today advise lowering fat intake and substituting polyunsaturated for saturated fats. Our initial excitement over the role of oat bran in reducing cholesterol has been dampened some by those now questioning its real value. More investigations are obviously going to be needed, but it certainly can't hurt to eat this natural food until we know for sure. It may well turn out that its benefit is an indirect one because it replaces some of the extra fat content in our diet, and that is what we should all be striving for. Bran cereals are just as filling and nourishing for breakfast as eggs, bacon, and buttered toast. To no one's surprise, food manufacturers are now jumping on the bandwagon concerning bran, fiber, and polyunsaturated fats. More health-inducing products are now available. As a consumer becomes more health conscious and more selective in his purchasing tastes, food producers do listen. For them it's a matter of economics!

However, if these do-it-yourself measures aren't working, you are definitely a candidate for one of the effective cholesterol-lowering drugs. These must be prescribed and followed by your physician.

Those with cholesterol problems should have their cholesterol levels rechecked at least yearly. And you may need to remind your doctor to test you at the time of your yearly routine exam.

8. Take One Aspirin Every Day
Research studies have confirmed that men and women over the age of fifty who take a single adult aspirin every other day or one baby aspirin every day have approximately a 40 percent reduction in their risk of heart attacks. And if aspirin reduces the risk of heart attacks, it will more than likely reduce the risk of strokes by a similar percentage.

9. Consider Hormone Replacement Therapy
Even though you may not have much in the way of menopausal symptoms, as soon as your periods stop, you would be wise to consider

beginning low-dose hormone replacement therapy (HRT), unless there exists a specific reason not to. Study after study has shown that estrogen reduces your risk of heart attack and stroke by as much as 50 percent.

There is one bit of reassuring news if you have already developed coronary artery disease. The damage can actually be reversed by any or all of the following: not smoking, eating a balanced low-unsaturated-fat diet, regular exercise, and daily baby aspirin. However, the most dramatic improvements come when estrogen replacement is used.

CANCER PREVENTION

When I was in medical school in the late 1950s, we were told that scientific research would within five years discover both the cause of and cure for all cancer. That monumental piece of optimism has obviously not come to fruition. It may never. But along the way medical science has offered improved surgery, chemotherapy, and radiation technology that have increased cure rates. Especially important has been technology that has made it possible to detect cancers at much earlier stages. So until the ultimate discovery of a cure for all cancers becomes a reality, we have to rely primarily on early detection to assure our best possible chance of cure. How can this best be accomplished?

1. Mammogram

There is probably no better example of the value of early discovery than with breast cancer, a disease that strikes one out of every nine women. The routine use of low-dose mammography has enabled us to find breast cancers before they are palpable. When discovered at this stage, not only do women have a greater likelihood of cure but cure without mastectomy. It can now be shown that lumpectomy with radiation therapy, which preserves the breast, offers cure rates equal to the traditional modified radical mastectomy.

It probably will take years for women to think of routine mammography in the same way as they now do about Pap smears. Mary tells me that of the women who come through the Menopause Center only one in three have ever had a mammogram. And of those who have had mammograms, too many have not kept up to date with them.

Women should have their first mammogram at age thirty-five (age thirty when there's a family history of breast cancer) and should repeat them every one to two years between the ages of forty and forty-nine. (These are standard recommendations. I personally encourage my patients to have one done annually after age forty. I base this on the recommendation of the renowned Swedish mammographer Dr. Laszlo Tabar of the Central Hospital in Falu, Sweden, who cites as his reason that breast cancers tend to grow faster during this decade—the forties—than in any other). After age fifty, mammography should be done annually. No excuses! Thirty seconds of discomfort is worth one year of peace of mind.

I also suggest to my patients that they stagger their annual mammogram with their annual medical exam (whether by a family practitioner, internist, or gynecologist). For example, if a woman sees her physician every January and has her annual mammogram every July, that means she will have her breasts examined by either a doctor or by X ray every six months. This, along with monthly self-examination of the breast, is the safest approach.

It's hard to convince women to perform regular self-examinations. Many don't because of the fear of discovering the "Big C." But that is really foolish thinking. Early discovery of cancer is crucial because it offers a high cure rate without the loss of the breast. That in itself should prompt all women to religiously examine their own breasts monthly, preferably after their periods or the first of the month if they no longer have periods.

2. Pap Smears

Cervical cancer is unquestionably a preventable disease. If women would have their Pap smears done on an annual basis, they could almost be assured of not developing the serious (called "invasive") form of cervical cancers. Yes, as the media has pointed out to us, there are some "false negative" Pap smears. But by doing them yearly and having them processed in a qualified lab, the risk of missing something important diminishes markedly because the natural history of cervical cancer is one that takes many years to arrive at the serious stage.

3. Pelvic Exams and Ultrasound

Ovarian cancer is one of the most serious cancers of the female genital tract. Only about one in four victims of ovarian cancer can be cured. The reason for this abysmal prognosis is because ovarian malignancies frequently do not cause symptoms (e.g., pain) until late in their stage of growth.

The pelvic exam is helpful in finding early

ovarian cancers but of limited value, especially in large women or in women who are difficult to examine pelvically. This is why pelvic ultrasonography, using the new vaginal probe, is now being used in special centers to pick up early ovarian cancers.

4. Bowel Checkups

Colon and rectal cancer also need to be detected early. After fifty, a rectal exam should be done at the same time a woman has a pelvic exam. I know it's uncomfortable, and no one likes it, but many rectal cancers and lower colon cancers can be found with just the physician's examining finger.

Starting at age fifty you should ask your doctor for a home test for blood in the stool. The presence of blood in the stool could indicate cancer somewhere in the gastrointestinal tract. Colonoscopy is advised every three to five years after age fifty.

High-fiber diets are associated with a reduction in the incidence of colon cancer, so it is wise to eat adequate high-fiber foods along with perhaps the daily use of the fiber supplement psyllium, such as Metamucil.

Cancer is not a pleasant topic. It causes all of us anxiety just talking about it. But it is no longer a death sentence. The hallmark of cure is *early* detection.

OSTEOPOROSIS PREVENTION

Osteoporosis is virtually 100 percent preventable. As discussed in chapter 6 (Estrogen and Osteoporosis), estrogen, exercise, and calcium supplements can nearly guarantee that a woman will not have to spend her latter years either hunched over or as a bedridden invalid.

How much calcium supplement a woman should take depends much upon her age and her dietary intake. A woman in her thirties and forties who is still menstruating should probably take 500 mg. of elemental calcium a day. Premenopausal women need 1000 mg., and postmenopausal need 1500 mg a day plus 400 I.U. of vitamin D.

VITAMIN SUPPLEMENTS

I don't think that anyone really knows for sure what the adequate requirement is for vitamin supplements. Our government has given us RDA (recommended daily allowances), but the question is, should we take even more than that, and, if so, how much?

It's an individual thing. Mary takes no vitamin supplements whatsoever and seems to feel as

BETA CAROTENE
(Pro-vitamin A)

25,000 I.U.

(rumored to reduce the risk of cancer)

VITAMIN B COMPLEX

1 cap/tablet

VITAMIN C
(rumored to prevent colds)

1000 mg.

VITAMIN E
(probably reduces the risk of heart attacks in both men and women).

200–400 I.U.

NIACIN TIMED-RELEASE CAPSULES
(proven to improve cholesterol values)

800–1000 mg.

ASPIRIN
(decreases the incidence of heart attack in both men and women)

1 baby aspirin a day

PSYLLIUM FIBER SUPPLEMENT *(Metamucil).*
(Fiber has been shown to reduce the incidence of colon cancer.)

1 rounded teaspoonful in a glass of water

BRAN
in the form of oat bran cereal or muffin

for breakfast or snack

good or better than I do—and I take them. We eat only fresh foods in our house, nothing canned or frozen (it's outside the house where junk food gets me in trouble!). For what it's worth, I'll share with you what vitamins and supplements I take every day (see page 220), admitting, however, that at least four of the items on my "list" are there only because of "scientific rumor" and not scientific proof.

THE KEY TO PREVENTION
Only a fool takes good health for granted; it can change instantly. But a mid-life woman can definitely increase the odds of having good health through preventive steps and basic body maintenance.

The key to preventive health measures is self-discipline. And that boils down to attitude. You must ask yourself how badly you want to feel better and live longer. How important is it to you? Is it worth giving up culinary delights? Is it worth exercising on a regular basis—even when it's the last thing you feel like doing? Is it worth taking vitamins and supplements? Is it worth trips to the doctor's office and having mammograms and Pap smears done on a regular basis? How much do you want good health and the good feeling that comes with it?

221

You are the one who will ultimately decide. As you do, keep in mind that others love and need you. You owe it to them as well as to yourself to maintain good health. Make it your goal to leave this world feeling as good as possible as late as possible.

TWELVE

❧

Making the Most
of Mid-Life

WHY not consider menopause as God's signal for you to take a good hard look at where you've been, where you are, and how you want to spend the rest of your life. This shouldn't be too difficult. After all, what time of our life is more introspective than mid-life as we realize our own mortality?

For many, menopause and mid-life can be a time of emotional swings and low self-esteem and uncertainty. You can do much on your own to stop this.

WHAT YOU CAN DO

Get Busy and Do Something
Many a woman in mid-life and menopause feels defeated, and the biggest obstacle in the

survival course of mid-life is herself. In order to cope, a woman has to take some action—any action. John Rosemond, a family psychologist in North Carolina, wrote in a syndicated column, "Self-esteem is synonymous with self-sufficiency, the ability to stand on one's own two feet. Self-sufficient individuals assume responsibility for their own happiness. Rather than depending upon others to make them happy, they discover the possibility of self-fulfillment." So get moving. Start by listing goals for yourself. Think of a talent, skill, or interest that you would enjoy, then pursue it and improve on it. Try something new. Accomplishment builds self-esteem. Maybe you've always wanted to learn how to play golf or tennis. Maybe it's dabbling in something creative like art, writing, gourmet cooking, or flower arranging. Consider a part-time job or a class at a nearby college. Get involved in a community or church activity. Anything. But get busy and do something that stimulates your mind.

Get Some Exercise

If you haven't exercised in the past, make time for it now! Consider swimming, or water jogging, biking, or low-impact aerobics. Incidentally, from a health standpoint, these energetic activities are not much better for you than brisk walking three times a week. So the exercise doesn't have to be much, just something. Let's face it, you're probably not going to make it into the Olympics! Of course, if you've been leading a sedentary life, then any degree of exercise feels like nothing less than masochism—beating up on your poor defenseless body. But soon the endorphins manufactured in the pituitary of the aerobically exercising individual treats the participant to a psychological "high." It will keep you coming back to the workout arena for more. Exercise is a wonderful way to work out those bottled-up emotions and to feel better about everything—including yourself.

Quit Comparing Yourself with Others

Everyone presents an image outside the home that defies the reality of what takes place inside the home. No one is as good as he or she may appear socially. Every person on earth is to some degree a hypocrite. It's natural for you to present your best side in a public situation. That's one of the reasons for looking well groomed and stylish. When you compare yourself to others, you are putting your real self up against the fictional image you have of other people. It's not a fair comparison. It simply makes matters worse and fosters the process of self-devaluation.

Find a Support Group of Other Women
A woman needs other women if she is to maintain a healthy self-image. A woman needs others with whom she can identify, someone to offer fresh new perspectives, someone she can confide in. We're talking about a support group, where fears can be shared and where women can kid and laugh about injured feelings and damaged self-esteem. Also, many women define themselves by the men around them—a husband or father, for example. A support group of other women can help a mid-life woman see herself independently of these male perspectives, and this can be a healthy contribution to the woman coping with menopause and mid-life.

Recognize and Accept Responsibility for Life's Disappointments
This seems like it's a negative exercise, but, in fact, it can be quite freeing. Put your failures behind you. It is a waste of time to point the finger of blame at people or circumstances in your life. Admit you made some bad choices or you were in situations over which *you* had no

control. Then get on with it. If you had a miserable childhood, that is regrettable. But stop letting it interfere with your future. The real issue is not who's to blame; rather, what are *you* going to do about it now? Keep telling yourself, "I am responsible for me!"

Dare to Take Risks

Don't scrap some activity or endeavor just because you think you're too old or because someone might make fun of you or criticize you for it. There will always be critics no matter what you do. That's because not everyone likes or appreciates the same things. Realize that whenever you take action, you might take some flak along with it. So be prepared for it. And don't let it discourage you. Too many men and women in mid-life stop trying new things, taking risks, and making choices, as if their lives were winding down. That's foolish, defeated thinking. Take the challenge to make something new, something more out of yourself. Take a risk, and try to enjoy the rest of your life!

A TIME FOR CHANGE

For the mid-life woman, menopause brings with it physical changes that have effects on her emotions and self-esteem. Hormone therapy, in time, can relieve some of these emotional problems. But too many women rely entirely on hormone therapy to renew them emotionally, psychologically, and spiritually. Much of the way a mid-life woman feels about herself comes from external sources, something HRT can do nothing about. As we have seen, mid-life is a confluence of life events. Many of them are endings—the departure of children from the home, the death of a parent, the loss of a friend. It then becomes essential for a woman to create new beginnings, to make new friendships and relationships, and to establish an exciting life for herself in her later years. For some this does not come easy; for others it will be a welcomed change.

A CHALLENGE FOR MID-LIFE

When most people think about their future, they focus on retirement and financial security, which is quite natural. Yet even though financial assurance is certainly an important consideration, in the total picture it is not—as so many who enjoy financial independence will testify. Christina Onassis, daughter of billionaire Aristotle Onassis, was quoted as saying, "Money does not bring happiness. Our family is a perfect example."

228

Two words that rich and secure people use most are "I'm bored." So there has to be more to retirement than just kicking back, relaxing, and playing with our "toys" (although it does sometimes sound pretty good to all tired, overworked people, including me!). A self-indulgent lifestyle that centers only on vacation homes, golf, travel, puttering around the house, and watching TV just doesn't cut it. It's a waste. Rarely does it bring long-term personal satisfaction. I hope these things can become a part of everyone's retirement, but a problem arises when they creep to the top of our priority list. There they have a way of changing us—and usually not for the better.

As a woman and her husband plan for their mid-life years, they should take great care not to allow them to become ones of self-pleasure and materialism. They did in the life of one man we know.

This retired gentleman is very wealthy. One day he sat at the bedside of a family member who was dying of cancer. The wealthy retiree lamented how empty and lonely his life had become and how all his luxuries were not bringing him the expected "happiness" he thought they would.

Unfortunately his time of reflection and introspection was short-lived. Minutes later he was talking once more about his ring and sports car he had just bought.

How then should we plan for our later years? The very first consideration should be given to how we want to live. Will it be for ourselves or for others—or for both? What will our priorities be?

Mary and I believe the best advice we ever received on the subject of priorities came from our eighty-six-year-old uncle—Dr. O. J. Finch— who shared with us in his home one day after having recovered from a serious stroke. "Kids," he said, "never forget this one fact. Life—and by that I'm talking about meaningful living—is relationships, and they are infinitely more important than things or position." Advice worthy of putting into practice.

It was this kind of wisdom our wealthy friend needed to hear when he sat by the bedside of his dying family member.

PUTTING OTHERS FIRST

We have talked a lot about the potential of estrogen to prevent medical problems. The best preventive medicine for the soul is to get involved in the lives of others. Relationships. When we're concerned about the needs of others, we have less time to worry about or feel sorry for ourselves.

Those who discover the importance of relationships have discovered the key to finding personal satisfaction, not just during the middle years but throughout life. The earlier a person learns this principle, the better off he or she will be. Being involved in the lives of others—being available and willing to help—is what creates a truly productive life. When others become more important than ourselves, it has a way of rekindling the flame in our soul. When we serve others, it exercises our mind, compelling us to think about ways to meet their needs. The result is personal contentment and inner peace.

Therefore, during mid-life as we make plans for our future years, those plans should include reaching out to others, putting them and their welfare before our own. This should become the life goal of the mid-life woman.

Some women may feel most comfortable touching the lives of others with their pen— writing letters or sending cards to friends or shut-ins. Others may choose to volunteer at the local soup kitchen or rescue mission or meals on wheels. You may feel burdened to spend time reading to sick children in a hospital or being with the elderly in nursing homes.

Commitment to others is how to make the middle and later years really count for something. It can also be therapeutic.

Janet was a distraught middle-aged widow who came to the Menopause Center for help. She had a son who fought valiantly in the Vietnam War. He came home a quadriplegic. For years he was confined to a wheelchair, totally dependent on Janet. She loved and cared for him as only a mother can do. But her son unexpectedly developed a liver disease and died.

The loss was devastating. Janet could not come to grips with her son's death. Each day was more painful and lonely than the one before. Severely depressed, she began a self-imposed confinement in her house. She would just sit alone and wish her son back in his wheelchair.

When she came to our center, Mary knew that we could help her physically—Janet was obviously in menopause. But the deep hurt in her eyes cried out for more than just hormones. She needed someone to come alongside and work with her. She asked for and went through counseling. In a very loving way, it was pointed out to her that the only way she was going to pick up the pieces of her life was to get her mind off of the tragic loss of her son. She needed to focus on others. That is precisely what she did. It was the cure.

She started by donating her son's wheelchair to a local charity. Then three days a week she volunteered in the children's hospital, reading and playing games with its young patients.

Janet found that the best prescription for depression and the best way to find peace and happiness is to get involved in the lives of others.

There is another bonus that we can expect when there is less of "me" and more of "others" in our life. It is a sharpened sensitivity to things around us—for example, nature. How often we take its beauty for granted. But when we are happy and content and our mind is less preoccupied with ourselves, there is more time to appreciate the natural beauty of this world—sunsets, the ocean's surf, little critters of the forest, flowers along the highways, starry nights, beautiful cloud formations, and, of course, much more. I believe that we lack the therapy of nature in our modern lives.

Mid-life is a most appropriate and beneficial time to appreciate beauty in great works of art—music, literature, and paintings. This is the time of life when we bring to art our own maturity and experience, and we can understand and feel many works of art more deeply.

Mid-life, at least its later years, should find us making choices about how we intend to live out our next thirty years. If we see an inappropriateness or imbalance to our priorities, then it is time for an immediate change, a time to realign our perspectives and readjust our visions for the future. It should be done swiftly, however, because changing the way we are inside becomes more difficult the older we get. Age definitely has a way of hardening the heart or making us apathetic.

TO RETIRE OR NOT TO RETIRE

As the mid-life woman nears retirement, some practical decisions will have to be made. If a woman loves her work and finds it personally satisfying, there may be no need to retire at all. But when she has the option to retire comfortably and her job or career has lost its zest and appeal, then it is time for a change. The mid-life woman should not feel hesitant about changing her work situation. Studies show that today people switch careers and jobs more frequently than they used to; in mid-life a brand-new career can resurrect a ho-hum, lackluster life.

234

New tasks, ventures, and ideas challenge our mind to grow. Oliver Wendell Holmes has been quoted as saying, "A person's mind, stretched by a new idea, never goes back to its original dimensions." That is why pursuing new careers, projects, and hobbies is so important. If we don't, we can get too comfortable doing "old folks" things long before our time—like staying home all the time, eating the same old foods, watching the same old TV programs in the same old chair, and spending time with the same old people.

Patty was a mid-life woman who was bound and determined she wasn't going to spend her later years in a rut. This charming fifty-five-year-old friend of Mary's owns a bakery here in town. One morning she came to our door delivering one of her special cakes for a bridal shower Mary was giving.

I happened to be home at the time, and I asked Patty why she started a business at this time in her life.

"Well," she said, "it wasn't a lifelong dream or goal or anything like that. It just sort of happened. My two daughters had college degrees, and neither knew what she wanted to do. I wanted to do something new and different, so we decided to combine our talents and money and start a small business out of our homes, baking carrot cake for health food stores. It wasn't long before friends asked us to bake ribbon cakes for their special occasions. I guess they were a hit. We soon outgrew our kitchens trying to keep up with the orders.

"So we found a little place downtown to rent, a hole in the wall really, and after a little paper and paint and elbow grease, it began to look quite presentable. We bought some used stoves and refrigerators from a nearby chicken pie restaurant, and we were ready to go. Now we've outgrown our little shop, and we're looking for a second location!

"I hire older women to work for us who need part-time jobs and who are energetic and like doing creative things."

Patty stopped for a minute, thinking. Then she continued, "When the girls left home to go to college, I looked around and saw how bored some of my friends were. The only thing some of them had to look forward to was buying a new dress for the next luncheon they would be attending. I knew that wasn't for me. I needed something both fun and challenging.

"It's hard work—baking—but I love the people who come into the shop. Customers are always interested in what we do. We talk like neighbors do over the fence about all sorts of things. Every day is different, and I especially enjoy being with my daughters. So mid-life for me has been special."

Age has little to do with ability. Age has nothing to do with vision, commitment, dreams, and accomplishment—things that keep us "young at heart."

DON'T PROCRASTINATE

The one thing that frightens Mary and me the most during mid-life is how quickly time rushes by. It seems summer is here and gone before we have the chance to even plan a day at the beach, let alone actually go. It seems no sooner are we taking down our Christmas decorations than we find ourselves at next year's Christmas tree lot picking out another one. So the last thing we should be doing during this time of our lives is procrastinating.

Dr. Kevin Lehman and Randy Carlson in their book *Unlocking the Secrets of Your Childhood Memories* (Thomas Nelson, 1989) tell the story of a man who was preparing for his wife's funeral after her sudden and tragic death. As he and his sister-in-law went through his deceased wife's dresser, gathering clothing to take to the mortician, he found a tissue-wrapped package of lovely lingerie that she had bought some eight or nine years before. It was made of exquisite silk and trimmed with lace, the impressive price tag still attached. His wife had never worn the lingerie. She had always said she was "saving it for a special occasion." As he slammed the bureau drawer, the grieving husband said, "Don't ever save anything for a special occasion. Every day you're alive is a special occasion!"

Lehman and Carlson admonish their readers not to "wait to make memories. Don't wait for some special occasion when you can stop to do what you've been postponing too long already. Remember: Tomorrow's memories are being made today."

Make new goals, but keep them as short-term projects that you can complete quickly. Lehman and Carlson cite one such goal. For example, say you decide to pass along something to your children for them to keep after you have died that will help them remember you by—something to help them better understand you and your perceptions about life. To accomplish that goal you might record an audio cassette or videotape in which you talk about your roots, your positive childhood memories, and the values you hold. Share from your heart what you consider important in life.

ATTITUDE

Attitude has so much to do with the success of our mid-life years. If we think old and talk old, we surely will be old. Mid-lifers should be vigilant not to allow their lives or their plans for the future to be boring. Simply stated, boring people are boring to be around.

The wise mid-life woman and her man should make every effort to keep the mind stoked with creative thoughts, always looking for interesting things to do. They should consciously strive to remain adventuresome, flexible, and able to keep an open mind. They should never say to themselves, *I'm too old to change,* or *I'm too old to do that!*

Much of our attitude about our later years is molded to some extent by others. For example, what we elect to do during our retirement years often gets "handed down" from our parents. However, what was good for them may not necessarily be good for us. We should plan to do what we want to do and not what others expect us to do.

A good attitude also includes looking at the humorous side of life. Don't get too serious about everything. Being able to laugh at life and ourselves makes us fun people to be around. This is something Mary has been able to do much better than I. I have a hard time in this area. Frankly, just writing down this admonition makes me squirm! Nonetheless, it is a good and important goal to strive for.

TO MOVE OR NOT TO MOVE

Another choice the mid-life woman or couple may be called upon to make is whether to stay in their home or move. When children leave, the house can seem large and empty.

Moving is not an easy decision. A lot depends on whether kids and grandkids will be coming to stay, in which case you'll surely need the room. Another consideration is that moving, unless it is nearby, means leaving a loyal and faithful circle of friends—your support group. That can be a great loss and not fully appreciated until after a move has been made.

On the other hand, your home may be partially or totally paid for. You may find yourself sitting on equity that can help you live more comfortably during your later years. This can be a good reason to sell and move. Moreover, a move can offer a new interest, a new project, a new excitement.

We have friends who moved away from Long Beach, where they were both born and raised. People thought they had flipped out. But they had fallen in love with another town and wanted to move there. It was not an easy decision. They first had to deal with the pull of their hometown and good friends. They started by asking themselves, "Do we live here because we really love Long Beach, or do we live here because we are just comfortably familiar with Long Beach?" They finally decided it was the latter. They made the move and have not regretted it for a minute. Yes, they had to make new friends, but they also have kept their old friends. They are now living where they really want to live. They dared to take the risk, as all of us should be able to do during our mid-life years.

THE JOYS OF MID-LIFE

Mid-life can be a woman's most joyous time of life—in fact the best years of her life! True, during the middle years life's obligations don't disappear, but it is not unusual for time, a once-precious commodity, to become more plentiful as the family grows up and leaves. Frequently these years are less hectic, less of a rat race, and a time to slow down a bit. As one of the most respected authorities on the subject of menopause, Leon Speroff, M.D., has said, "Mid-life can and should be the start of something good . . . never the beginning of the end."

Often mid-life can be a time to explore untapped creativity. Cheryl, a forty-three-year-old mother of two teenage girls, was challenged by her husband to fulfill a lifelong dream. So she blocked off one afternoon a week and took painting lessons. Her dreams became more than dreams. She was able to uncover a natural talent she wasn't aware she had. Cheryl had a good sense of color and an ability to capture her subject in an impressionistic way on canvas. Today she displays and sells her oil paintings in a Newport Beach art gallery.

Sometimes in mid-life a woman discovers a new activity in old clothing. Mary Anne is the mother of four daughters, all of whom are married. Few people have had more experience planning weddings than she. So she put that experience to work. Mary Anne now owns and operates her own wedding coordinating business out of her home. She has the joy of planning these special events without having to foot the bill!

Mid-life offers a woman the freedom to change. This is the time she no longer must stick to the same time schedules, the same routines that shaped her life when the children were home. Change makes life interesting. It keeps us out of ruts. It keeps us from getting bored. We know one couple who in their mid-life years began investing in run-down houses and apartment buildings. He does the repairs and remodeling; she collects the rent and pays the bills. This has allowed them to buy a motor home. Because they now have more time, they can pick up and travel anywhere they want to—which, of course, includes visiting their children. Before they overstay their welcome, off they go again. This couple made significant changes and improved their lives. For them, *boredom* is a word that doesn't even exist in their vocabulary.

Mid-life is often the time of life when our children have children. What a blessing grandchildren can be! What fun it can be to just sit back and enjoy the wonderful and amusing things they say and do. What fun it is to reexperience little arms around your neck, cuddling, building things with blocks, bedtime stories—all the things you recall about your own children when they were little.

We know of one grandmother of seven who decided she had read enough books to her grandchildren that she could write her own. She hired an art student at a nearby college to do the illustrations, and she then submitted the manuscript and artwork to a publisher. It was accepted. She is now working on her third book. No pressure, no stress. Just creative fun.

Mid-life is also a time to surround yourself with people you like, a time to expand your circle of friends, a time to become close to those you trust and feel comfortable with. It is a time to travel and go places with friends, see places you've never seen before and only dreamed about. It is a time in which you can pursue theater arts, community affairs, new sports activities, and charitable organizations that reach out to the needy.

Mid-life is a time when a woman can do more than just exult in her past experiences and accomplishments. It can be a time to put into use these rich resources—all that she has learned over the years from raising children, from her job and career, and from her knowledge of social situations and convention.

It is possible for *every* mid-life woman to say of her mid-life experience, "These are the happiest and most productive years of my life."

244

SPIRITUAL REJUVENATION

The emotional turmoil of the mid-life years frequently uncovers a woman's spiritual needs. She may find it just as necessary to get help for spiritual ills as it is to get treatment for her physical and emotional infirmities.

Dr. James Dobson, in his outstanding audiocassette tape called "An Understanding Look at Menopause," says it best: "All the emotions that surface during a woman's menopause have a spiritual side to them." He points out that "the mind, the body, and the spirit are very close neighbors, and one usually catches the ills of the others!"

Perhaps you are now going through mid-life and menopause—struggling as Mary did. Or maybe you are better prepared than she was—thinking ahead and making plans for your future. In either case, I would simply suggest to you this one thing we learned from Mary's experience: If you have been neglecting the spiritual side of yourself, have been "spiritually dry" for some time now, then do something positive about it. We live in a time when so much emphasis is given to the material aspect of our life. So many people believe their only real problem is they don't have enough money to enjoy life or have a big enough house or a good enough job, when actually their real problem is that they don't have enough appreciation for what God has already given them.

I believe it is important, especially as you deal with menopause, to realize that you are more than just a female body and hormone system. We are all spiritual beings with a need for more than physical and material comforts alone. We need spiritual companionship that only God can provide.

THIRTEEN

❧

A Word to Husbands

COUNSELING women for menopause frequently reveals a great deal about the husband at home and the state of a marriage.

"The patient you're seeing next, Bob," Mary was telling me one day, "is a real classy lady—designer clothes, pretty, sweet, but depressed. I think she's lonely. I suspect it's more than just menopause. If you've got the time, you may want to hear her whole story. Your next patient is late anyway."

As Leslie entered my consultation office, I could see what Mary meant. She appeared to be about fifty. She was perfectly groomed, right down to her well-manicured fingernails. On her left hand was an enormous diamond, tastefully mounted in a pavé setting.

I complimented her appearance, but she didn't respond. She seemed preoccupied and withdrawn.

"We'll be talking about menopause today, Leslie, but before we do, I'd like to ask you if there are any other things going on in your life that concern you."

She spoke hesitantly at first but began to recount some things about her life with her husband. "Bill and I have been married for thirty years now and love each other very much," she said. "But lately I feel that we've lost that . . ." She thought for a minute, then continued, ". . . that special intimate relationship we once had. Sometimes I wish we were starting all over again. In those days we struggled financially, and the kids drove us crazy, but at least we were together. Bill and I used to really talk back then. But no more. I'm not sure why. He's very successful, and we have all the things we ever dreamed of having, but it doesn't mean a thing because we don't talk anymore. I feel I'm on a merry-go-round and helpless to get off."

I could sense Leslie was beginning to relax. She seemed relieved to be talking about her feelings openly. She continued, "Bill and I have something going on every weekend. Our friends say we give the most unusual and fun parties of all. As a group we'll often cruise to Baja, California, or Catalina on our boat. Sometimes it's skiing, or we'll organize a golf or tennis tournament in the desert—always something competitive. When I say *we* set it up, I really mean Bill sets it up—or rather his secretary. Then when all the arrangements are made, he tells me about *our* plans. He never asks what I'd like to do. He rarely asks my opinions about anything. He just assumes. He seems obsessed with keeping our lives busy.

"Bill really means well. He's a good man and is good to me. It's just . . . something is missing.

"One time a friend asked me, 'What do you do all day in that big fancy home of yours?' And before I could open my mouth to answer, Bill said, 'Leslie can do anything she wants in that home. It's her castle.'

"But I just wish Bill could understand how lonely my 'castle' is. Even though I don't have to lift a finger to keep it up, I feel like a prisoner there. Everything is done for me.

"During the week I have luncheons, play tennis, golf, and go to movies with my girlfriends, but it seems now as if I'm just going through the motions. What I really need is someone to talk to, someone who will listen to me, someone who understands me."

I asked Leslie if her husband was aware she was in menopause and coming here for help.

She said, "I mentioned that I wasn't feeling well, but I don't think he really heard me. He never asks how I feel. I don't seem to be an important part of his life now that the children are gone. It seems I'm just part of the package he has to manage, like his business. But I desperately need some part of him to survive, to give me a reason for living.

"Now that I've told you all this, Dr. Wells, I feel like a big crybaby. I guess I should be grateful I have a husband who takes care of me. He is kind and loving."

I suggested to Leslie that perhaps she and her husband didn't have much private time together.

"You're right," she said. "The only time we're together is bedtime. When I ask him anything about his work or try to confide in him about a problem I'm having, he pats me on the arm and says, 'We're both tired. We need to get some sleep. We'll talk about it tomorrow.'

"Well, I've had too many tomorrows with no talks. I miss the intimacy we used to have. I miss the fun we had when the children were with us—at least we communicated.

"It seems he'll do anything to avoid talking

about meaningful things or reminisce about stuff we used to do. My theory is that Bill is scared of growing old, and I think that's why he's got us in the fast lane—so he won't have to think about getting older. He really is obsessed with cramming everything in. It's as if time is running out, and he is forcing me to be a part of his frantic efforts to do things. But I don't want all that junk in our lives. I just want him!"

It didn't take much on my part to identify several major deficiencies in their marriage, one of them being her husband. She seemed to have a pretty good understanding of her own situation. She was in menopause—our tests showed that. Though her symptoms were mild, they constantly irritated her and made it more difficult to cope with the relational problems she obviously had with her husband.

The most prominent shortcoming of their marriage, however, was that her husband simply wasn't talking with her or listening to her. Bill had difficulty spotting his wife's "change of life" more than likely because he was so engrossed and involved in his own mid-life crisis.

THE "TBL" PRINCIPLE

Adele Lawrey, M.A., our Menopause Center's licensed marriage and family counselor, tells husbands in session that there are three things every wife needs from them, especially if they are going through menopause. She calls these three the "TBL" principle of marital health. The *T* stands for *Talk*. The *B* stands for *Be*. The *L* stands for *Listen*. Men, your wife may be taking hormone pills, but that's only half the problem. You're the other half.

From time to time Mary and I speak to young couples about what makes a good marriage. Drawing from our own thirty-five years of marital experience, we share both the good and bad, the mistakes along with successes. On many occasions Mary asks the men in the audience, "How many of you men learned from your mothers how to treat women? I'm not just talking about sex, but how to love and appreciate a woman."

Usually very few hands go up. This is unfortunate. Every man would do well to learn from a woman how to treat a woman. Our mothers are "experts" on this subject. Sometimes, unfortunately, they know how it is to be mistreated by a husband. In many cases they have been well treated and know the things a woman appreciates. Either way mothers are the best advisers. A man who as a child has been an eyewitness to the husbandly "art" of treating his wife is fortunate indeed.

What a man learns from his mother is simple. A woman wants her husband to talk with her, be with her, and listen to her.

"I DON'T NEED TO TALK"

There are two reasons that confiding is not an easy task for most men. One is because a man's ego nature fights to keep everything inside, to avoid outside help, and to rely upon his own instincts and abilities. Second, men tend to compete and achieve. That is why job and career so often climb to the top of his priority list. And it is in the workplace where he discovers that keeping his mouth shut about his personal life protects his position better. A man soon learns that being a good poker player pays off and improves chances for advancement. The reason for this is that in the job's atmosphere of competitiveness, any "weakness" he shares about himself may be used later against him in the "courtroom" of company politics. Thus, the "I don't need to talk" philosophy.

This closed-mouth tendency is particularly characteristic of men and not women. In fact, when was the last time you ever heard of a husband saying to his wife, "Honey, we never talk anymore!" That's the wife's classic line, isn't it? Women have little difficulty expressing themselves. By nature they prefer to talk things out; their orientation as primary caretakers is relational. They do not mind being transparent.

Unfortunately men bring this reserved, tight-lipped trait home with them. The one who cares about him the most—his true confidante—gets shut out. Wives are the ones who must prod their mates to talk. Wives are deeply affected and hurt when they get shut out. As one patient told me, "My husband comes home, eats, sits in front of the TV, and hardly says a word. I'd welcome any conversation—about his job, what he did that day, what irritates him—anything."

Men, your wife wants you to talk with her. If she hurts inside and you don't talk with her, she feels abandoned and alone. She sees her situation as hopeless. This is true in all marriages, for all men and women. But it is especially true when a woman is going through menopause.

What a woman doesn't need to hear from her husband is, "What's the matter with you lately!" Rather, a genuinely concerned husband will state just those changes he actually sees. Our counselor Adele calls these the "I" messages: "Honey, I see you are more irritable and nervous lately. I get the feeling something's bugging you. Maybe it's just me, the way I'm seeing things, but I'm concerned about you." In other words, it's not an attack, just an observation. Then what a woman needs to hear is, "I don't understand what you're going through, but I wish I could do something to help you feel better."

Immediately you have just removed one great burden from her shoulders—the thought of going through this ordeal of menopause and mid-life alone. That one statement gives her hope in an otherwise hopeless situation. She needs to *know* you care.

For the mid-life marriage to flourish, each of you must be privy to the other's needs and feelings. That means communication. That means talking with each other (not at each other). But if you, her best friend, hold everything inside and refuse to share with your wife your own fears and concerns, she is unable to support or encourage you. Neither can she advise you. So in your silence you risk losing your best resource of human help.

Yes, there are normal hindrances to husband-wife communication. They're called kids. A friend of mind said, "You know, when I come home at night I would just love to sit down and talk with my wife. But it's craziness in my home. Kids are screaming at each other; two of them arguing over the phone. Another pounces on me for the keys to the car. The youngest wants me to critique her cheerleading routines. How do you have meaningful communication with your wife when it's like a zoo at home?"

It's hard. Sometimes you can't. But you have to try. Especially as a husband, you have to make an extra effort to communicate, to talk, and to confide. Perhaps a simple solution is an hour later in the evening when the kids are settled down in their rooms and you and your wife can be alone. Exhausted perhaps, but alone. Maybe then you can talk with each other intimately.

There are two other kinds of men who have trouble communicating but in a different way and for a different reason.

The "executive workaholic" does not suffer from being silent. He is the Type A personality who in fact never stops talking. From the moment he opens the front door at night he talks and talks—but only about one subject, his work. This man shuts his wife out of his heart just as surely as his taciturn counterpart.

Then there is the husband who doesn't share meaningful things with his wife because "she wouldn't understand." What an egotistical and erroneous assumption. In fact, not only would she understand, but because of her own inner-circle perspectives, she is probably the one most likely to give the best advice.

A wife is usually the best adviser about things because she knows her husband better than anyone else. She also has his best interests at heart. Whether a man realizes it or not, his wife happens to be his most-prized earthly possession, his best source of wise counsel. The man who talks with his wife only about trivial matters is not only rude and condescending but is also foolish.

A husband who learns (and it is a learning process for men) to overcome these problems does himself a great favor. To illustrate how thoughtful some husbands can be, let me tell you about a close friend of mine, a contractor. He and his wife and Mary and I were driving back from a five-day fishing trip we'd been on together. He was driving. His wife was in the front seat with him. I could see that he was thinking about all the things he had to do when he got home. He turned to her and said, "Honey, I need your help and understanding the next few days. I've got lots of work ahead of me and won't be with you as much as I'd like to be. But I'll do my best to be home as much as possible."

Meaningful communication occurs when both parties feel the freedom to express themselves without being interrupted or judged. The goal should be to preserve the sanctity of each other's thoughts, feelings, and attitudes.

THE INVISIBLE MAN

One of the great needs of a married woman is intimacy with her husband—both sexual and nonsexual.

I believe that when it comes to intimacy, men are basically dense. Men usually will not see the development of an intimacy gap in a relationship as quickly as their wives. In fact, men are really quite oblivious when it comes to spotting discontent in their spouses. I never learned this in medical school, but I am convinced that women are born with a special "antenna" that has an uncanny ability to detect relational dysfunction, especially as it relates to romance in their life. This is something men don't have, perhaps because as a rule men do not easily open up emotionally to other people.

Yet intimacy is essential to a marriage relationship. A woman needs it and knows she needs it. A man needs it but doesn't know he needs it.

Intimacy requires taking time to be with

someone. The everyday "rat race," the tread-mill upon which we huff and puff, is one of the great deterrents and inhibitors of marital inti-macy. Time together when your life is busy and cluttered is rarely intimate. Take again, as an example, this chapter's opening story—the way Bill took it upon himself to plan and ar-range "their" schedule, cramming everything in. Oh yes, he and Leslie were together, but they were not alone together. The result was that emotionally they moved farther and far-ther apart.

Couples need to be with each other a lot. You can't have quality time without quantity time. I've heard busy husbands say, "I'm not home a lot, but when I am home I spend quality time with my wife." That's hogwash. Small talk is often the breeding place for heart-to-heart is-sues. Moments of silence can be preambles to meaningful dialogue.

It is our responsibility as husbands and fathers to keep our priorities straight and not allow our jobs to interfere with family time. It is our job to see that a substantial part of that time is private, that we are alone with her. Bill always had to have people around when the two of them were "together."

One thing Mary and I found very valuable

was a regular date night. We tried to set aside one night a week to go out together for dinner and talk. Yes, much of the conversation focused on the kids and how they were getting along, but even when we were talking about the children, important things were said about our relationship with each other. Just the fact that we were out together was valuable. No interruptions. No phone. No beeper. No calls from the delivery room. Just the two of us.

Intimate moments alone and together can be therapeutic for the menopausal wife. Where there is a conducive atmosphere to speak frankly and candidly, she will feel the freedom to admit some of the feelings she has been having, such as feeling unlovely, unappreciated, not for what she does but just for who she is. She needs her own identity.

Intimacy also requires a sense of romance.

I'm not talking just about sex now. Sex is only a part of romance. Romance may or may not lead to sex and, in the case of women, may be even more meaningful when it doesn't. Also, a lot of men think that romance is simply making their wives feel good, buying them flowers or candy, or making them happy in some way. Those things are nice, but they're often not the genuine thing.

I believe romance means two things—creativity

and involvement. A woman perceives something to be romantic when she sees that a man has spent time doing something for her that takes some creative thinking or requires a commitment or extra effort from him. For example, for a man to buy his wife a box of candy is not necessarily a romantic gesture, especially if, say, he was able to buy it quickly and easily at the airport on his way home from a business trip. However, a box of candy might be perceived more as a romantic gift if a man goes out of his way to a special confectioner's store to buy a particular candy that he knows is his wife's favorite. Romance is not the thing itself. It's the thought and effort behind the thing.

I must admit here that I speak as a man who has himself been lacking in this area. Too often I'd dash to the nearby Hallmark store or flower shop on the very day of Mary's special occasion. She knew it was last minute. (Mary tells me I am improving, but then she tacks on the word *some*.)

Sometimes I do plan spontaneous surprises. Without telling her in advance, I spring on Mary a night out or weekend away at a spa, hotel, or mountain cabin. She sometimes says, "Oh, we can't do that," but she does, and we love it. Mary is no different than many women—she loves surprises.

Intimacy also involves physical touching. Again, we're not talking about sexual touching but rather a physical sense of closeness. This means touching and snuggling. It includes hugs and squeezes and smooches—more than those routine pecks that become part of the everyday routine. Christian author and speaker Gary Smalley suggests that a wife needs between eight and twelve hugs or touches every day to feel secure and loved. And every woman wants to be hugged and caressed until *she* is ready to let loose.

In short, intimacy is the art of "being there," in mind and body. It is during these times that a husband is granted his greatest opportunities to reach out and tenderly offer encouragement to his wife in words and deeds. For the mid-life woman to hear her husband say, "I love you. You are beautiful to me. You are the most precious thing in my life," is more therapeutic than all the estrogen ever manufactured.

LISTENING, NOT JUST HEARING

Two men were talking one day. One of them said, "My wife talks to herself a lot." His friend answered, "Mine does too, but she doesn't know it. She thinks I'm listening."

Unfortunately, this is all too true of many

marriages. A man can be *hearing* what his wife says but not *listening*—attentive or involved in what she's saying. Sometimes a man will put up the appearance of listening but may not be listening at all.

A woman needs her husband to listen to her. This may not be true of all married women but perhaps especially true of the mid-life woman. In mid-life, after years of marriage, it is easy for a husband and wife to become accustomed to the patterns of each other's communication and make assumptions about how the other will react. In the process they cease to really listen to each other. Dialogue breaks down.

Just as talking and sharing is difficult for husbands, listening doesn't come easy either. When a man comes home at night, he is usually tired, emotionally and physically. He's been talking to people all day, and he wants to switch off his communication center. If his wife is also a part of the work force, she probably feels the same way. So when two communication systems shut down, he will probably receive less flak for his indifference.

There is a different kind of challenge when a woman works at home. She's been alone all day; he's been with people all day. By 6:00 P.M. she is a veritable storehouse of information and questions and is ready (and needs) to unload it all immediately before she forgets. He enters the house and is exhausted and tired of people. If the woman is in the throes of menopause, she may be so emotionally charged that she won't see or care that her husband is wasted from fatigue. In other words, the estrogen-deprived wife may "pounce" on her mate before he has a chance to relax and "come down."

Personally, "coming down" means opening my mail, sitting down on the couch, propping my feet on the coffee table, and watching a brief synopsis of the day's news on TV. Then I'm ready for quality listening. I'll then sometimes say, "Start with the good news first, Mary."

Quality listening is not easy. It takes energy because it demands concentration. Our mind must be cleared of all other preoccupying thoughts. Listening includes eye contact. Listening is awareness of body language that communicates things other than what's coming from the lips. If a wife says, "It's no big deal," yet her arms are tightly crossed, her neck is stiff, and she has that certain look in her eyes, it usually means it really *is* a big deal! When it comes to listening, the optic nerve is as important as the auditory nerve.

A husband may face two other problems that

impair his listening ability at home. First, he may be preoccupied with work or business problems. There may be a strained relationship at his job that bugs him. Or finances may worry him. Preoccupation with such pressures is unnecessary when couples share their problems, but for men, that's not easy to do. A wise wife who senses preoccupation in her mate will prepare him ahead of time: "Honey, I need to talk with you later about something." She should add, "Not anything major. Whenever you can give me some time."

Second, the husband of a woman in menopause who has not yet started on hormone replacement can begin to grow weary of her mood swings and emotional outbursts. He might start to tune her out. But his mental retreat does not go undetected. His wife will pick up on it and become even more distraught. She may even lash out openly, attacking and blaming the things she sees separating the two of them (and very often things he personally enjoys). But her oral flurry is frequently coated and layered with exaggeration. "All you ever do is watch television" (not true, he does do other things). Or, "You're always puttering in the garage" (again an overstatement of facts). And, "All you ever think about is your work!" (again exaggerated).

265

The bristling attackee tunes out the attacker. With each raid it becomes easier not to listen. He probably doesn't hear her parting shot, "You never talk with me either."

In summary, you may be transformed into a poor listener when you are tired, preoccupied, or attacked. But it doesn't have to be that way if you can learn to listen effectively to the woman in your life.

Your wife needs you. She needs you to talk with her, she needs you to be with her, she needs you to listen to her. If you don't, there could be a price to pay. Where there is a void in a woman's life that only you can fill, and you don't fill it, fantasies or affairs may become her only recourse.

"WALKING ON EGGSHELLS"

Lowell is a corporate engineer, a person used to having things run smoothly and efficiently. He is also used to fixing things. At home the sink stops up; he fixes it. At work a business glitch threatens a deal; he fixes it. But menopause was an enigma to him, for it defied his fixing expertise. His wife burst into tears for no reason at all. Her moods were up and down like a roller coaster. He looked for an explanation, but everything seemed about the same. One day this strong, controlled husband could take it no longer. "What in the world is going on with you?" he shouted out in frustration, which succeeded only in bringing more tears of hurt and humiliation.

Perplexed husbands react to the mystery of menopause in various ways. Some men realize something is wrong and encourage their wives to seek medical advice. Too many others, however, lash out in anger, not really at their wives, but at the strange, nebulous, seemingly unfixable force that causes her to behave this way. Some husbands, seeing their once composed and stable companion suddenly swinging from emotion to emotion, envision all retirement plans going up in smoke. They get depressed and withdraw.

Then there are men like Bill, whom we discussed earlier, so desperately dealing with their own mid-life crisis that they remain oblivious to their wife's mid-life experience and the trauma of menopause.

A husband who suspects his wife is in menopause should encourage her to see the doctor as soon as possible. If her doctor's exam and blood tests determine that she is not in menopause, well, that's good too. It will save a lot of time and expense running from doctor to doctor trying to find an organic reason for her symptoms. Just as important, it lets your wife know you care. You haven't abandoned her. That means so much to a woman. Mary, who interviews all the patients who come to the Menopause Center, tells me that the most common complaint she hears is that the woman's husband just doesn't seem to care about or understand what she's going through.

If a woman is in menopause, there are two things her husband needs to keep in mind.

First, be prepared for emotional outbursts. During these times your wife may say terrible things to you, things that have been pent up for a long time. Maybe they have not ever surfaced before because she's always been busy raising the kids. But now that they have left the home, the lowered estrogen in her system may prompt her to spew forth things that have festered for years. I'd like to say not to take them personally, that they are not from the heart but from the glands, and that she can't help it. But the truth is that sprinkled throughout her catharsis are real feelings that have been bothering her for some time. So you can't ignore them. Even her most stinging words may be on target. There may be areas in which you could improve.

Therefore, don't react defensively. Look at it constructively. Weigh her words even if they are being shouted. She is giving you insightful and valuable clues.

As you "learn" from her, stay calm, but don't be so noticeably controlled that even that will upset her. You walk on eggshells, my friend, when a woman's hormones are out of whack. One thing I can tell you is it will be much easier once she is on hormone replacement.

Second, don't fall into the trap of thinking that all emotional symptoms and outbursts that appear in mid-life are hormonally generated. Even when menopause has been diagnosed as the offender by her physician, there are situational stresses that contribute to her emotionalism. One of those stresses may be you. When you can reduce your contribution to her stress, you will certainly make her doctor's job much easier and her "cure" that much faster.

BEING SENSITIVE TO THE WOMAN IN MENOPAUSE

It is important for you as husband to be sensitive to what your wife is going through in menopause and mid-life.

The mid-life woman is often at a crossroads both physically and socially: Old activities and relationships are ending, new ones may not yet have begun. She may feel lost, uncertain, afraid. After years of having an identity as a mother, she may no longer feel she has a clear identity. She wonders who she is and what she should do. A man needs to be sensitive to his wife's search for a new identity in mid-life.

Frequently mid-life is a time when past problems—even childhood problems—surface in a woman's life. A husband needs to be sensitive to his wife's past experiences and how they affect her present.

Mary was raised in a home with one sister and no brothers. Her parents came from the old country and had a more provincial attitude regarding modesty and sex. It wasn't their fault. They were the product of their parents' attitudes, just as we all are to varying degrees. Mary tells the rest of the story:

> *Bob grew up in a home where bathroom and bedroom doors were seldom closed. But my family was ever so modest and proper about things. I remember when my sister and I were shapely teenagers, my father was always telling us to put clothes on as we ran from the*

bathroom to the bedroom. We were wearing either a full-length slip or nightgown, but for him that wasn't enough!

My family's modesty was ingrained in me when Bob and I were married. I felt the need to keep myself modestly covered even in front of my own husband. This created a real friction between us during our early years of marriage. Believe it or not, I even dressed and undressed in the closet!

It took major attitude changes on my part to overcome this shyness about my body. Today I constantly remind myself that God created my husband and me for each other, and that I have nothing to be ashamed of. When I see the effects of age taking place in my body—the wrinkles and sags—I remind myself that Bob has them, too. So I no longer consider age a negative in regard to my self-image. I've finally come to realize that we are all in this aging pickle together. So with that in mind, I decided once and for all to throw caution to the wind—along with my flannel nightgowns—and let Bob enjoy the woman he married.

A husband needs to be sensitive to the insecurities of his wife that might stem from her childhood. These insecurities may emerge in the first year of marriage, as with Mary and me, or they may come out later, during the turmoil of menopause.

Open discussion is the key. Again, it's the TBL principle—talking, being, and listening.

FOURTEEN

❧

Answers to Your Questions about Menopause and Mid-Life

QUESTION 1: I have decided to go on hormone therapy, but I want to do everything possible to reduce any risk there might be. What would you suggest?

ANSWER: First, have your doctor keep the dosages low, yet still adequate to keep you free of menopause symptoms. The progestin dose should be sufficient to protect your uterus from estrogen stimulation without uncomfortable side effects to you. As we learn more and more about progestin, it appears the *length* of time it is taken each month is the important factor (e.g., twelve days) and not necessarily the dose.

Therefore, it is possible to use very small dosages of progestin.

If bone and cardiovascular protection is your goal, most authorities recommend at least .625 mg of conjugated estrogen (Premarin).

Second, I would recommend that you have your blood estradiol (the amount of estrogen circulating in your blood) tested occasionally, perhaps every few years. Timing is very important for the evaluation of a blood estradiol. To assure consistency and reliability, it should be drawn twenty-four hours after your last estrogen pill (or midway between the patch or injections). Optimally the blood level should range between 60–100 pg/ml. Many authorities feel comfortable with 150 pg/ml for the high side. When it is very high, some patients paradoxically get the very *same* symptoms they would have when it is low and in menopause range. If it is less than 60, then you are not getting your money's worth for health protection.

Trying to find the ideal dosage of those sometimes annoying progestins is tricky. If the dosage gets too low (even though still capable of protecting the uterus), you may experience some light bleeding from a fragile unstable uterine lining. To date, there is no meaningful blood test to "monitor" progestin as we now have for estrogen.

And finally, be health vigilant. Examine your breasts every month. Be faithful to get annual mammograms after age forty (or earlier if there exists a strong family history of breast cancer). Be sure to have a pelvic exam and breast check once a year. It has been shown time and again that your self-exam is important, but your mammogram and doctor's breast exam are more productive in picking up early breast tumors. Annual medical exams also enables your doctor to "fine-tune" your HRT when needed. These precautions alone can erase most of the fears you may still be harboring about risks hormones may impose on you.

As I pointed out earlier in the book, try to stagger your annual mammogram with your annual medical exam. In that way every six months your breasts are either being examined by X ray or the doctor. Just a little extra assurance.

QUESTION 2: I tend to get migraine headaches. Can I take estrogen therapy?

ANSWER: I do *not* consider migraine headaches to be a contraindication to hormone replacement therapy. There are many "triggers" that bring on migraines. One of them appears to be a fall in blood estrogen levels. This is seen midcycle at the time of ovulation, just before a period, and, of course, at menopause.

If the blood estrogen level can be kept stable without the peaks and valleys, the risk of bringing on a migraine headache is minimized—*if* the migraine is hormonally induced.

By going on *daily* estrogen therapy the migraine sufferer will minimize the estrogen "ups" and "downs," thereby possibly reducing frequency and intensity of the migraine "attacks."

That is why I try to avoid putting any migraine patient on the cyclic method of hormone replacement (see chapter 4, Hormone Replacement Therapy) since it calls for five days off estrogen. During the "off" time many will experience migraines.

Menopause expert, Dr. Leon Speroff, M.D., supports this clinical observation and says, "Patients with migraines are good candidates because many do better on HRT."[1]

Dr. Lila Nachtigall, M.D., of New York, who has been treating menopausal patients for decades, does not hesitate to give estrogen to her migraine patients but prefers estradiol rather than conjugated estrogens feeling estradiol increases blood flow to the brain better than other forms of estrogen—a "plus" for migraine sufferers.

QUESTION 3: I'm fifty-three years old. My last period was more than two years ago. Recently I have noticed a loss of bladder control. Is this related to menopause?

ANSWER: Very possibly. Leaking urine with coughing, laughing, sneezing, or exercise (stress incontinence) is an embarrassing and annoying symptom. Some women even curtail activities because of it or resort to wearing a pad during the day to avoid an accident. This kind of incontinence worsens with age because supporting tissues around the bladder become weakened with the loss of estrogen, resulting in what we call the "unstable bladder." Estrogen replacement, either with pills, patches, or injections without or preferably along *with* estrogen vaginal cream, often improves this kind of stress incontinence and in some women corrects it altogether. What a nice substitute for surgery!

In some instances (usually the result of childbirth) the bladder will drop down. This is a condition known medically as cystocele. It creates an anatomical disturbance that is so great that estrogen will not help. In these cases surgery is necessary to correct the condition.

QUESTION 4: How long must I take hormones once I begin?

ANSWER: Most authorities feel that once started, hormone replacement should be continued to at least age seventy for cardiovascular protection and even beyond to maintain strong bones. It is the opinion of many osteoporosis experts that estrogen's bone protective ability continues even beyond age seventy-five.[2]

Were a woman to stop taking estrogen before age seventy-five, the stripping of calcium from bones could begin again at the same rate she would have experienced had she never taken estrogen. Her future risk of osteoporosis fractures with this resumption of calcium stripping would depend on the status of her bone mass at that time (easily determined by bone density testing).

Generally, a woman feels so much better on long-term estrogen that she usually doesn't want to stop (and those that do usually see the difference and return to its use). The additional 2.6 years of quality life that the estrogen user enjoys is a good motivator for continued long-term use.

Another reason to continue taking hormones for life is the possibility that they may help to maintain one's ability to think better. Now who wouldn't be interested in that?

Researcher Dr. Barbara Sherwin of McGill University, Montreal, Canada, has been testing cognitive skills in the elderly for many years. She has concluded that some aspects of cognitive thinking, i.e., short-term memory and the ability to learn new things, is enhanced as the result of estrogen therapy.[3] This suggests that estrogen may play an important role in cognition and that hormone replacement might delay or postpone the inevitable loss of cognitive functioning that invariably comes with age.

Perhaps related to mental acuteness is the finding of Dr. Stanley Birge, reporting at the 1993 North American Menopause Society, who said that elderly estrogen users sustained fewer injury-type falls than nonusers. Is it because their reflexes are faster? Probably.

And finally recent research by Dr. Victor Henderson of the University of Southern California suggests estrogen may even reduce the risk and symptoms of Alzheimer's disease—just more mounting evidence of the long-term benefits of estrogen.

As medical scientists learn more about HRT, more specific recommendations will be available regarding the length of time hormones should be taken.

QUESTION 5: I am seventy years old. I've never taken estrogen. Should I start taking estrogen now?

ANSWER: The answer is probably yes, in order to take advantage of estrogen's bone protection and the possible mental benefits it may confer. Cardiovascular health improvement has not been shown to be one of estrogen's benefits after this age.

But the price of starting hormone replacement therapy may be bleeding, at least initially. The likelihood is small but present. It is easily correctable.

However, you must keep in mind that if you arrive at age seventy and are still healthy, you probably have good genes, and from an actuarial standpoint, your life expectancy is good with or without estrogen. It is a decision you should make with your doctor.

QUESTION 6: I am forty-three years old and still having periods. What is the best contraception for me?

ANSWER: Most women in their forties are anxious to be done with contraception techniques.

Who can blame them? But women do get pregnant in their forties. In fact, I had one patient who had a baby at age forty-six!

For premenopausal mid-life women there are several good methods of contraception available. Which one is chosen is an individual matter and can be selected because of convenience or on the basis of its known failure rate. The following are some of the current methods of contraception starting from the most protective to the least.

1. Sterilization.

This is available for either the male or the female. For a man, a vasectomy can be done in the doctor's office under local anesthesia and is usually less expensive than a woman's tubal ligation. However, many men harbor misgivings about what it might do to their future sexual "performance." If any apprehension does exist, though totally unfounded from a scientific perspective, this option should not be chosen.

Sterilization for the woman can be done immediately after delivery (postpartum tubal ligation) or at the time of a caesarean birth. It can also be accomplished in the nonpregnant state using a laparoscope—sort of a straight surgical "periscope"—that is inserted, with the patient asleep, through the navel and, along with a supplementary device, burns through each tube. This method is often referred to as the "Band-Aid" procedure because the incision is so small. Though generally not a risky procedure, it does require a general anesthetic and a short stay (usually a few hours) in the hospital. It is also more expensive than a vasectomy.

To date, there are no statistically significant long-term effects with either vasectomy or tubal ligation. I am impressed with the number of women who appear to have more irregular bleeding and pelvic pain after tubal ligation, but to my knowledge this has not been satisfactorily confirmed by research studies.

2. Birth-Control Pills.

The next most effective means of contraception for the premenopausal woman is the birth-control pill, often referred to as an oral contraceptive (OC). They are virtually 100 percent effective in preventing pregnancy. Though it was once thought that OCs might contribute to cardiovascular disease and should be stopped at age forty (age thirty-five for smokers), this is no longer true. The new low-dose OCs are safe at any age and can be taken even into the fifties.

Many authorities now recommend using OC until age forty-five to fifty and then switching over to hormone replacement therapy (HRT). This is a reasonable and convenient approach that will probably become very popular in the future, especially in light of the proven benefits of OCs, i.e., prevention of osteoporosis, ovarian and uterine cancer, pelvic inflammatory disease, and benign breast disease.

The safety of the birth-control pill for older women has come about as the result of a dramatic decrease in dosages. Drs. David A. Grimes and Leon Speroff, at the 37th Annual Clinical Meeting of the American College of Obstetricians and Gynecologists, said that "oral contraceptives have undergone dramatic changes in the past thirty years resulting in approximately a fourfold decrease in estrogen doses and a tenfold decrease in progestin doses." They also pointed out that oral contraceptives reduce the incidence of ovarian cancer by 40 percent, which is wonderful news considering the fact that "ovarian cancer has the poorest prognosis of all gynecologic malignancies."

Drs. Grimes and Speroff addressed head-on the issue of whether birth-control pills caused breast cancer and concluded, after a rather exhausting review of the studies on this subject, that "all studies undertaken thus far have failed to find an increased overall risk of breast cancer with the use of oral contraceptives." They did note that one study done by The Centers for Disease Control CAHS found an increased incidence of breast cancer in women who had an onset of their first period at a very early age and a history of taking OCs many years—again during the days when high-dose type OCs were the only ones available.

So, like low-dose hormone replacement, the birth-control pill does not seem to increase one's risk of breast cancer and can be used by middle-aged women for very effective contraception.

Incidentally, the birth-control pill, being a combined estrogen and progestin in one pill, provides relief from menopausal symptoms as does HRT. However, the need for birth control notwithstanding, HRT is preferred over the oral contraceptives for control of menopausal symptoms because, being far less potent, HRT causes far fewer side effects.

3. Barrier Techniques.
The next most protective method of birth control are barrier contraceptives, a category that includes the highly protective intrauterine device

(IUD). The copper IUD ParaGard is a particularly good method of contraception for the mid-life woman, offering a failure rate of around one percent—rivaling even the oral contraceptive.

The popularity of the other barrier methods have recently enjoyed a resurgence, buoyed by the finding that they can help to prevent sexually transmitted diseases, including the much-dreaded AIDS virus. These spermicide-containing preparations and devices include vaginal foam, diaphragms, suppositories, sponges, etc., all of which are "over the counter." Their disadvantages are their failure rates, which can range from 10 to 20 percent. A not-so-insignificant consideration, too, is the fact that they do interfere with sexual spontaneity. These barrier contraceptives are a good choice for the menopausal woman when ovulation becomes less frequent, considerably decreasing her fertility.

4. Natural Family Planning.

Finally, many women become proficient with the use of natural family planning, but its success is directly proportional to a woman's experience in understanding her own cycles. Because a premenopausal woman experiences menstrual irregularity, pinpointing the intermittent ovulations becomes quite a task.

QUESTION 7: I am forty-five years old. I have been on hormones two years for the treatment of menopausal symptoms. I am taking them in such a way that I have planned periods—much like the birth-control pill. My doctor says that HRT does not assure I won't get pregnant. How can I know when I no longer need contraception?

ANSWER: Your doctor is right. HRT is not to be considered contraception. What HRT is treating—menopause—eventually is, however.

In the past, a woman was not considered sterile until one year had passed after her last period (that's a long time to wait while suffering menopausal symptoms). But in the instance where hormone replacement is being used and inducing periods artificially, how can she know when she is sterile from menopause? Easy. She should ask her doctor to order a FSH blood test. FSH is the hormone test that diagnoses the presence or absence of menopause (see chapter 3, Understanding Menopause). If the FSH remains in the menopause range (according to that lab's criteria) on two occasions six months apart, that woman can safely scrap her contraceptive methods. This still applies if she is on oral contraceptives for both menopause and contraception. In this instance, the FSH should be drawn on the last pill-free day, in other words, one day before she starts a new packet of pills.

QUESTION 8: I am forty-two years old and had a hysterectomy for endometriosis. They also removed my ovaries. Since surgery everything has changed. I've been depressed. I have no energy. I have not the slightest interest in sex, and that's new for me. I wish now I'd never had the operation. My doctor has prescribed every kind of estrogen, but it just hasn't helped. I'm not the same person I once was. What can I do?

ANSWER: I've heard this story from too many women to dismiss it as one individual's psychological problem. There are many possible explanations, but the one I consider most plausible is the failure to replace testosterone as well as estrogen when the ovaries are removed.

In chapter 10 (Sexuality in Mid-Life) we talked about the fact that ovaries produce testosterone as well as estrogen. Therefore, it seems only logical that testosterone should also be replaced along with estrogen when the ovaries are removed. Surgical menopause imposes an even greater *decrease* in testosterone production than does natural menopause. The reason is that during natural menopause the testosterone production diminishes gradually.

The sudden loss of testosterone from surgery can be associated with significantly more psychological changes than natural menopause. Research studies show a greater incidence of depressive symptoms, for example. Therefore, it makes good sense that younger women who have had their ovaries removed should have both their estrogen *and* testosterone replaced.

The benefits of testosterone may include: (1) reduction in the appearance of depressive reactions; (2) heightening of sexual interest, excitement, initiation, and response; and (3) increased energy levels and an enhanced feeling of well-being. These benefits, not surprisingly, should pique the interest of other women, too—those who have gone through natural menopause.

It is a research-documented fact that testosterone and estrogen replacement used together enhance the overall well-being of surgically menopaused woman better than when estrogen is used alone.[4]

So, in your case, perhaps testosterone is the missing ingredient that would help. Ask your doctor to prescribe testosterone *in addition* to your estrogen. The most ideal and convenient combination of estrogen and testosterone is found in Estratest, manufactured by Solvay. However, I think testosterone injections work better for improved libido and, since they by-pass the liver, may even be safer.

Progesterone is also produced by the ovaries, *but* it ceases when ovulation ceases, and its replacement is less essential in most women. However, testosterone production continues even past menopause, so it makes sense that it too should be replaced, especially in women like yourself who are struggling postoperatively.

What are some other reasons why women can go down emotionally after hysterectomy? In some cases, the patient has not been properly prepared for what hysterectomy would mean to them. Some may subconsciously feel that hysterectomy is the final toll of the bell, an unwelcome reminder that they have lost their childbearing potential, a substantial portion of their femininity, and their youth. If not discussed preoperatively, it can be a factor postoperatively.

Another explanation for feeling different after surgery is not unique to hysterectomy. Depression and letdown frequently follow any type of major surgery. There is a great deal of apprehension and worry as the surgery date approaches. When the procedure is over and all has turned out well, there can be an emotional "sag."

The other suggestion I would make is to be sure that you are adequately absorbing the estrogen into your system. Have your blood estradiol checked (see question 1).

QUESTION 9: I am forty-eight years old. My doctor has had me on the daily method of HRT for eight months now, but I still bleed all the time. What would you recommend?

ANSWER: The daily method of taking estrogen and progestin is very popular, but it is better reserved, I think, for women over fifty or those who have been sometime without a period. If a woman's ovarian function is still present, it is almost impossible to override, and attempts to do so almost always result in persistent irregular bleeding that is discouraging. It is like beating a dead horse!

I would recommend that you have an office

biopsy of the uterus to rule out any other serious cause of the bleeding. If none is found, go back on the cyclic method of HRT (see chapter 4, Hormone Replacement Therapy). This will bring planned regular periods by working along with your own hormonal cycle. After a few years you can try the daily method again.

QUESTION 10: Will taking estrogen help my skin?

ANSWER: To a limited degree. But we must keep in mind that it is always difficult to distinguish certain body changes (such as dry skin) resulting from estrogen deficiency from those of the normal aging process. We have something to help the former but no "hormone" for the latter!

Many women who go on hormones do describe a feeling of smoothness and softness of their skin. They will often comment, "My skin is not as dry as it used to be." Their opinion is supported by at least one research study that showed estrogen may well retard some of the "aging" process of the skin, such as its thinning and, yes, those dreaded wrinkles.[5] They were able to show that estrogen in postmenopausal women tended to restore the skin's natural turgor and strength both by increasing its water content and by adding to it more collagen (a protein-supporting tissue).

But let's not forget one important fact—whether women take estrogen or not, wrinkles are going to come. The bottom line is that there are no wrinkle-free rides for anyone in this world—short of surgery. Ironically enough, more men than women choose to have wrinkle-removing plastic surgery these days.

QUESTION 11: I am fifty years old and was just diagnosed as being in menopause. I have gained twenty-eight pounds in the last five years. Is weight gain a part of menopause, and once I begin hormones will I lose it?

ANSWER: I wish that I could answer yes, but such is not the case. Women do have an increase in weight that comes at a time when their estrogen levels are falling. Whether the two are related is something we simply do not know.

As we all get older, the tendency is to eat out more often (that means more calorie-rich foods) and get less physical exercise. All this takes place at a time our bodies need fewer calories.

By that time we have developed a secure and

comfortable lifestyle that does not include cutting back on those calories. It seems that about every five years we all move to a new weight plateau. Unfortunately, mid-life weight does not come off with the ease it did in younger years!

Were we actually to reduce our caloric intake, it is very likely that we would avoid that insidious weight gain that comes with age.

If estrogen deficiency played a significant role in weight gain, we could expect that replacing that estrogen would shed those extra pounds. But this is not the case, at least in our experience. This is admittedly disappointing. Perhaps estrogen's failure in this department is explained by the fact that women on estrogen notice a sense of well-being, and when they feel well they eat well—just like men.

So as good as HRT is, don't anticipate that it will help you lose the creeping poundage you notice during the middle years.

In summary, if estrogen helps you reduce, count yourself lucky. But don't count on it!

QUESTION 12: I am forty-eight years old. I know I'm having menopausal symptoms, but my family doctor won't prescribe hormones for me because I'm still having periods. He also says he doesn't believe

in giving hormones, he says, because their safety has yet to be proven. What should I do?

ANSWER: Because of indiscriminate use of estrogen in the past, physicians got into trouble when some of their patients developed uterine cancers. When that happened, doctors simply stopped prescribing estrogen altogether and have been reluctant to restart. The reason for their reticence is, I'm sad to say, largely medical-legal. We do live in a litigious age, and unfortunately many of the medical decisions made today are done with the thought of avoiding courtroom entanglements.

But I believe more women will have access to hormone replacement therapy from now on with the safety of HRT being more firmly established.

In your case, I would recommend that you ask your doctor to order the blood test for menopause called serum FSH. If it comes back elevated and in the menopausal range, then you are menopausal. At that point, if you choose hormone replacement to relieve your symptoms, you have every right to have it prescribed for you. If he still won't give you hormone replacement, then go to a physician who will.

It is going to take a few more years for many doctors who found themselves recoiling from estrogen's past notoriety to feel comfortable prescribing estrogen once again. But the medical literature they are now reading is bulging with practical, for the most part trustworthy, information that emphasizes both the simplicity and safety of hormone replacement. I suspect it will not be long for all doctors to be able to prescribe HRT with confidence, especially to those women who *choose* to go on it.

I emphasized the word *choose* because, as mentioned in this book many times before, Mary and I strongly believe that it really is a woman's choice, one a woman makes after being accurately informed of the risks and benefits of estrogen. No one should "force" someone to take hormones. Neither should anyone "prevent" someone from taking them.

So if your doctor continues to say no to you, find one with an open mind—someone with an interest in menopause. They can be located in your area. Dr. Wulf Utian, founder of the North American Menopause Society and currently president of the International Menopause Society, has done us all a great service by compiling a regional list of U.S. doctors interested in helping menopausal women. A doctor near you can be found through the North American Menopause Society: 29001 Cedar Road, Suite 600, Lyndhurst, OH, 44124 (216-844-3334).

QUESTION 13: **The last time I refilled my estrogen prescription my pharmacist prescribed a generic drug for me. I've noticed a few hot flashes, and I'm beginning to feel the same way I did before I started hormones. Do you think the generic is the reason I feel the way I do?**

ANSWER: Very likely. Dr. Paul Doering, professor of pharmacy practice at the University of Florida College of Pharmacy, at a meeting I attended in Arizona stated that one out of every four drugs being dispensed in the U.S. today is a generic.[6] Cost naturally is a big factor in the proliferation of generics. In an attempt to save money some insurance plans are even forcing the substitution of generic drugs.

At the May 1–4, 1988 meeting of the American College of Obstetrics and Gynecology, it was pointed out that generic hormones are too often subpotent (by as much as 30 percent) and are frequently not therapeutically equivalent to their brand-name counterparts. This may be because government agencies and state laws have become too lenient on generic drug companies who tend to skimp on quality controls to keep costs down.

What does the use of generics mean to a woman on HRT? It means that she may be getting one-third less of the hormone she's paid for. It means that one-third less gets into her bloodstream. And it means she may be getting one-third fewer benefits.

If you are taking hormones for relief of the more immediate symptoms of menopause, like hot flashes, night sweats, and insomnia, you would be more likely to discover being "shortchanged" by a generic since you'd experience no improvement or loss of it once established.

But if you were taking estrogen for its long-term benefits to prevent the development of osteoporosis and cardiovascular disease, you might not even know the difference. You could be thinking you're practicing preventive medicine, but in reality you're not!

Because of this, I would advise you to insist that your pharmacist give you a brand-name drug when it comes to hormones. It may cost more, but it's worth it. Sometimes we as physicians forget to write "no generics" on the prescription. So as your doctor is writing out your prescription for hormones, ask him to note this. Then also check with your pharmacist that you are getting a brand name.

QUESTION 14: I am taking estrogen along with progestin that my doctor prescribed, but I still have hot flashes, and I'm still anxious and tense. I thought hormones would stop this. What's happening?

ANSWER: There are several possibilities. First, check to see if you are taking a generic form of the hormone. In the case of estrogen, be sure it is a trade name item like Premarin, Estrace, Ogen, Estratab, or Ortho-Est. So often women come to the center, and that's the only problem they have. All we do is substitute a trade name for the generic, and frequently the symptoms disappear.

Sometimes women on oral estrogen who continue to have menopausal symptoms can be helped by simply increasing the dosage of the pill. Unfortunately, there are limits that, when exceeded, can result in unpredictable and annoying bleeding.

Another possibility is that the estrogen is not being absorbed. In other words, it goes into your mouth and stomach, but perhaps because of too much acidity in your stomach, it is not being fully absorbed. This situation is easily diagnosed by determining a blood-estrogen level (serum estradiol). See question 1 as to how this test is to be timed.

If the blood-estrogen level is low, it probably means that you are what we call a "nonabsorber." This can be corrected by the use of a nonoral route such as the Estraderm patch, estrogen injections, estrogen vaginal cream, or even estrogen pellets inserted under the skin (not universally available in the U.S. because they are not yet FDA approved). These nonoral routes place the estrogen directly into the bloodstream, thus bypassing the faulty bowel-absorbing mechanisms.

Another reason for persistent emotional symptoms despite being on estrogen could be that your symptoms are due to stress—external and situational—and not from estrogen deficiency, even though you are going through menopause. The *reason* for the stress should be explored while you continue to take your brand-name hormone replacement therapy.

Finally, other non-estrogen reasons for hot flashes include thyroid disorders, alcohol abuse, acute anxiety attacks, and very rare tumors, such as carcinoid or pheochromocytoma (I've never seen either one of them).

QUESTION 15: I am fifty-two years old and developing a small light-haired moustache and even some peach fuzz on my face. This is terribly embarrassing to me. Why is this happening, and what can I do about it?

ANSWER: What you describe is actually very common during a woman's menopausal years. It is explained by the observation that up to 75 percent of estrogen production is lost after menopause or surgical removal of the ovaries, while at the same time only 50 percent of circulating testosterone is lost. This means there is proportionately more androgen "hanging around" than estrogen. This imbalance between the two results in an androgen dominance and the potential for increased hair growth (hirsutism), especially on the face. This will lessen with estrogen replacement.

However, if increased hair growth becomes progressively severe, your doctor should be made aware of it.

QUESTION 16: My doctor just diagnosed me as being in menopause. One of the most disturbing symptoms I have is mental confusion and memory loss. Will they get better as I take estrogen?

ANSWER: In our experience you can expect some but limited improvement in these two areas. Memory loss is also closely tied to stress and busy schedules (kind of like the absent-minded professor), and when things calm down some, memory will often be noted to improve.

QUESTION 17: Are the estrogen and progesterone used in HRT natural or synthetic? Where do they come from?

ANSWER: Estrogens used in HRT are natural. This means they either come from natural sources or their chemical formula is identical to hormones manufactured in the body. The estrogens are derived from various sources, including Mexican yams and pregnant mares' urine. Another popular natural estrogen is made in the lab, ending up with a chemical formula identical to estrone, the chief estrogen in postmenopausal women.

In contrast, the progesterone component in HRT is entirely synthetic and does not have the same chemical structure as progesterone produced by a woman's ovaries. The synthetic progesterone is called *progestin*. It is readily absorbed from the gastrointestinal tract, and it is this property that has made it far superior to the earlier forms of natural progesterone. Progestins are the only oral progesterones now FDA approved.

However, natural progesterones (which incidentally are made from Mexican yams and soybeans) have recently been micronized, a process that enhances their absorption.

They are not yet FDA approved, but I believe they soon will be. A few pharmacies will make up this natural, micronized progesterone for patients. I find it very suitable for patients who do not tolerate the progestins that traditionally have been used (see chapter 4, Hormone Replacement Therapy).

QUESTION 18: I am forty-six years old. When I was thirty-four, I had a hysterectomy because of persistent bleeding from fibroids. I have never had to take hormones, and I'm feeling very good. Since I don't have periods, how will I know when I go through the menopause, and should I consider taking estrogen?

ANSWER: An excellent question. It applies to lots of women who have had hysterectomies without the removal of their ovaries. First, I believe the process of menopause is speeded up some as the result of hysterectomy. The reason for this is unclear, but many physicians feel that during the removal of the uterus, the surgery is also taking away its small but sometimes significant contribution of oxygen-rich blood to the ovary. It is suspected that this very slight compromise of blood to the ovary may induce an earlier aging process of the ovary, which, of course, results in earlier menopause. So in your case you might expect menopausal symptoms to be making their appearance about now.

But remember, as many as 25 percent of women have few if any symptoms when they go through their menopause. You may be one of those. My suggestion for you and all mid-life patients who still have ovaries but no uterus is that you periodically (say, every year or two) have a blood test for FSH done. When it drifts up into the menopausal range, then you might consider taking estrogen for its preventive medical qualities (discussed in chapters 5 and 6).

On the other hand, if and when you begin to experience some of the physical or emotional symptoms of menopause (discussed in chapter 3, Understanding Menopause), you might consider the use of estrogen at that time; the FSH test becomes of only academic interest.

Your next decision would be whether to continue the estrogen into your senior years for its preventive medicine potential. But again, that is a matter of personal choice after looking at the pros and cons of hormone replacement and arriving at your own decision, one with which you can feel comfortable.

REFERENCES

Chapter Two: Emotions, Self-Esteem, and Stress

1. Jean Lush with Patricia H. Rushford, *The Emotional Phases of a Woman's Life* (Old Tappan, N.J.: Fleming H. Revell Company, 1987).

Chapter Three: Understanding Menopause

1. R. G. Wells, "Flashes, Flushes, and Night Sweats," *Senior Patient* (June 1990).

Chapter Four: Hormone Replacement Therapy

1. R. G. Wells, "Should All Postmenopausal Women Receive Hormone Replacement Therapy?" *Senior Patient* (January/February 1989): 65–67.
2. R. Don Gambrell, Jr., *Estrogen Replacement Therapy,* 2d ed. (Dallas: Essential Medical Information Systems, Inc., 1989).
3. B. Hillner et al., "Postmenopausal Estrogens in Prevention of Osteoporosis," *American Journal of Medicine* 80 (1980): 1115–30.
4. R. G. Wells, "Hormone Replacement Before Menopause," *Postgrad Med* 86 (1989): 61–71.
5. B. Staland, "Continuous treatment with a combination of estrogen and progesterone: A way of avoiding endometrial stimulation,"

Acta Obstetrics and Gynecology of Scandinavia 130, Suppl. (1985): 29–35. Also see B. Ettinger, "Optimal use of postmenopausal hormone replacement," *Obstetrics and Gynecology* 72, Suppl. (1988): 31S–36S. Also see R. G. Wells, "A Plan for Giving Hormone Replacement Therapy to Postmenopausal Women," *Senior Patient* (January/February 1989): 68–70.

Chapter Five: Estrogen and the Cardiovascular System

1. M. J. Stampfer et al., Prospective study of postmenopausal estrogen therapy. Ten-year follow-up from the Nurses' Health Study. *New England Journal of Medicine* 325 (1991): 756. Also see Trudy Bush, "Cardiovascular Mortality and Non-Contraceptive Use of Estrogen in Women," *Circulation* 75 (1987): 1102–09. Also see A. Paganini-Hill et al., "Postmenopausal estrogen treatment and stroke," *British Medical Journal* 48 (1992): 276–308.
2. T. W. Meade and A. Berra, "Hormone Replacement and Cardiovascular Disease," *British Medical Journal* 48 (1992): 276–308.
3. P. Greenland et al., "Mortality after Myocardial Infarction," *Circulation* 83 (1991): 484–91.

Chapter Six: Estrogen and Osteoporosis

1. J. C. Gallagher et al., "Effect of Progestin Therapy on Bone," *American Journal of Medicine* 265, no. 15 (1991): 171.

2. B. Ettinger et al., "Postmenopausal Bone Loss Prevented with Low-Dosage Estrogen and Calcium," *Annual of International Medicine* 106 (1987): 40–45.

Chapter Seven: A Matter of Choice—Yours

1. J. J. Bitter, "The Cause and Control of Mammary Cancer in Mice," *Harvey Lectures* 42 (1947): 221–46.
2. D. R. Gambrell, Jr., *Estrogen Replacement Therapy,* 2d ed. (Dallas: Essential Medical Information Systems, Inc., 1989), 88–91.
3. D. R. Gambrell, Jr., *The Female Patient* (April 1993): 50–62.
4. M. J. Stampfer et al., Prospective study of postmenopausal estrogen therapy. Ten-year follow-up from the Nurses' Health Study. *New England Journal of Medicine* 325 (1991): 756.
5. D. R. Gambrell, Jr., "Decreased Incidence of Breast Cancer in Postmenopausal Estrogen-Progestin Users," *Obstetrics and Gynecology* 62 (1983): 443–45. Also see Gambrell, *Female Patient* (April 1993), 50–62.
6. Lila Nachtigall et al., "Incidence of Breast Cancer in a Twenty-two-year Study of Women Receiving Estrogen-Progestin Replacement Therapy" *Obstetrics and Gynecology* 80 (1992): 827–30.
7. D. N. Strickland et al., "Relationship between Breast Cancer Survival and Prior Post-menopausal Estrogen Use," *Obstetrics and Gynecology* 80 (1992): 400–04. Also see L. Bergkvist et al.,

"Prognosis after Breast Cancer Diagnosis in Women Exposed to Estrogen and Estrogen-Progestogen Replacement Therapy," *American Journal of Epidemiology* 130, no. 2 (1989): 221–28. Also see R. D. Gambrell, "The Menopausal: Benefits and Risks of Estrogen and Progestin Replacement Therapy," *Fertility and Sterility* 37 (1982): 457–74.

8. T. L. Bush, "Risks of Cardiovascular Disease," *Transition* 2, no. 1 (Winter 1991): 4–6.

9. L. Speroff, "From OC's to Replacement Therapy: A Strategy for Transition," *Dialogues in Contraception* 2 (1989): 3.

Chapter Eight: Alternatives to Estrogen

1. F. Kronenberg, "Giving Hot Flashes the Cold Shoulder without Drugs," *Menopause Management* (April 1993): 20.

2. M. Hammar et al., "Physical Exercise and Hot Flashes," *Acta Obstretrics and Gynecology of Scandinavia* 69 (1990): 409–12.

Chapter Nine: Breast Cancer Patients and Estrogen

1. Physician poll, *Ob/Gyn Forum* 4, no. 3 (1989).

2. G. G. Ribeiro, "Carcinoma of the Breast Associated with Pregnancy," *British Journal of Surgery* 73 (1986): 607.

3. A. G. Wile and P. J. DiSaia, "Hormones and Breast Cancer," *American Journal of Surgery* 157 (1989): 438.

4. P. J. Maguire, *Journal of Reproductive Medicine* 3 (1993): 183–85.
5. North American Menopause Society Proceedings, San Diego, 1993.
6. D. R. Gambrell, Jr., "Decreased Incidence of Breast Cancer in Postmenopausal Estrogen-Progestin Users," *Obstetrics and Gynecology* 62 (1983): 435.

Chapter Ten: Sexuality in Mid-Life

1. William H. Masters, M.D., and Virginia E. Johnson, D.Sc. (hon), "Sex and the Aging Process," *Journal of the American Geriatric Society* 29 (1981): 385–90.
2. James Dobson, *What Wives Wish Their Husbands Knew about Women* (1975; reprint, Wheaton, Ill.: Tyndale House, 1978), 129.
3. Masters and Johnson, "Sex and the Aging Process."
4. R. L. Young et al., "Comparison of Estrogen Plus Androgen on Libido and Sexual Satisfaction," *Abstract of North American Menopause Society* (September 1991): 103.
5. B. B. Sherman et al., "Postmenopausal Estrogen and Androgen Replacement and Lipid Concentrations," *American Journal of Obstetrics and Gynecology* 156 (1987): 414.

Chapter Fourteen: Answers to Your Questions about Menopause and Mid-Life

1. L. Speroff, "Hormone Replacement Therapy," *Contemporary Ob/Gyn* 37, no. 11 (1992): 90–130.

2. B. Hulka et al., "Health After Fifty," *Patient Care* (September 30, 1992): 5–15.
3. B. Sherwin. "Estrogen and Androgen Therapy and Cognitive Thinking," *Psychoneuroendocrinology* 13, no. 4 (1988): 345–57.
4. G. A. Bachman, "Estrogen-Androgen Therapy for Sexual and Emotional Well-Being," *Female Patient* 18 (July 1993): 15–24.
5. M. Brincat et al., "The Long Term Effects of Menopause and Effects of Hormones on Skin," *British Journal of Obstetrics and Gynecology* 92 (1985): 256–59.
6. P. Doering, "Long Term Effects of Estrogen Deprivation," speech presented at the Central Regional Conference, Scottsdale, Arizona, February 1990.

INDEX

❦

A

B

C

Index

Index

H

Hair 2, 14–16, 39, 192, 300

HDL–C 100–101, 103, 105, 212

Headache 57, 276

Heart 5–6, 9, 19, 42, 57, 67, 81, 84, 97–99, 101–102,
 104, 106, 136, 140, 143, 160, 185, 204, 206–207,
 211, 213–214, 220, 234, 237, 239, 256–257, 259, 268

Heat 57, 60

Hernias 204

Hirsutism 300

Hormones 6, 11, 24, 28, 32, 35–36, 49, 51–53, 55–56, 64,
 66–68, 74, 80–81, 84–88, 90, 92, 94, 98, 103, 105–106,
 120, 126–129, 131, 133–134, 137, 146–147, 151, 177,
 190–191, 196, 213–214, 227–228, 246, 252, 265, 269,
 273, 275–276, 278–280, 283–284, 286, 291, 294–295,
 297–299, 302, 304

Hot flashes 56–57, 59, 61–62, 67, 80, 139, 146–149,
 151, 162, 296–299

HRT 66–68, 74, 78, 81, 85, 87–95, 125–126, 128,
 130–133, 138, 140–141, 143–144, 147, 150, 158, 214,
 228, 275–276, 279, 283–284, 286, 290–291, 293–295,
 297, 301

Hygiene 184

Hypertension 140, 205, 209–211

Hypothalamus 21, 51, 58–59

Hysterectomy 49, 74, 76, 86, 94, 287, 289–290, 302

I

Impotence 195

Incest 44

Insomnia 25, 60, 62, 67, 139, 297

P

R

S

Index

T

Other Living Books Best-sellers

400 CREATIVE WAYS TO SAY I LOVE YOU by Alice Chapin.
Perhaps the flame of love has almost died in your marriage,
or you have a good marriage that just needs a little spark.
Here is a book of creative, practical ideas for the woman who
wants to show the man in her life that she cares. 07-0919-5

ANSWERS by Josh McDowell and Don Stewart. In a
question-and-answer format, the authors tackle sixty-five
of the most-asked questions about the Bible, God, Jesus
Christ, miracles, other religions, and Creation. 07-0021-X

BUILDING YOUR SELF-IMAGE by Josh McDowell and Don
Stewart. Here are practical answers to help you overcome
your fears, anxieties, and lack of self-confidence. Learn how
God's higher image of who you are can take root in your
heart and mind. 07-1395-8

COME BEFORE WINTER AND SHARE MY HOPE by
Charles R. Swindoll. A collection of brief vignettes offering
hope and the assurance that adversity and despair are
temporary setbacks we can overcome! 07-0477-0

DR. DOBSON ANSWERS YOUR QUESTIONS by
Dr. James Dobson. In this convenient reference book,
renowned author Dr. James Dobson addresses heartfelt
concerns on many topics, including questions on marital
relationships, infant care, child discipline, home management, and others. 07-0580-7

THE EFFECTIVE FATHER by Gordon MacDonald. A practical study of effective fatherhood based on biblical principles.
07-0669-2

FOR MEN ONLY edited by J. Allan Petersen. This book
deals with topics of concern to every man: the business
world, marriage, fathering, spiritual goals, and problems of
living as a Christian in a secular world. 07-0892-X

FOR WOMEN ONLY by Evelyn R. and J. Allan Petersen.
This balanced, entertaining, and diversified treatment covers
all the aspects of womanhood. 07-0897-0

GIVERS, TAKERS, AND OTHER KINDS OF LOVERS by
Josh McDowell and Paul Lewis. Bypassing generalities
about love and sex, this book answers the basics: Whatever happened to sexual freedom? Do men respond differently than women? Here are straight answers about God's
plan for love and sexuality. 07-1031-2

Other Living Books Best-sellers

HINDS' FEET ON HIGH PLACES by Hannah Hurnard. A classic allegory of a journey toward faith that has sold more than a million copies! 07-1429-6 *Also on Tyndale Living Audio 15-7426-4*

HOW TO BE HAPPY THOUGH MARRIED by Tim LaHaye. A valuable resource that tells how to develop physical, mental, and spiritual harmony in marriage. 07-1499-7

JOHN, SON OF THUNDER by Ellen Gunderson Traylor. In this saga of adventure, romance, and discovery, travel with John—the disciple whom Jesus loved—down desert paths, through the courts of the Holy City, and to the foot of the cross as he leaves his luxury as a privileged son of Israel for the bitter hardship of his exile on Patmos. 07-1903-4

LET ME BE A WOMAN by Elisabeth Elliot. This best-selling author shares her observations and experiences of male-female relationships in a collection of insightful essays. 07-2162-4

LIFE IS TREMENDOUS! by Charlie "Tremendous" Jones. Believing that enthusiasm makes the difference, Jones shows how anyone can be happy, involved, relevant, productive, healthy, and secure in the midst of a high-pressure, commercialized society. 07-2184-5

MORE THAN A CARPENTER by Josh McDowell. A hard-hitting book for people who are skeptical about Jesus' deity, his resurrection, and his claim on their lives. 07-4552-3 *Also on Tyndale Living Audio 15-7427-2*

QUICK TO LISTEN, SLOW TO SPEAK by Robert E. Fisher. Families are shown how to express love to one another by developing better listening skills, finding ways to disagree without arguing, and using constructive criticism. 07-5111-6

REASONS by Josh McDowell and Don Stewart. In a convenient question-and-answer format, the authors address many of the commonly asked questions about the Bible and evolution. 07-5287-2

THE SECRET OF LOVING by Josh McDowell. McDowell explores the values and qualities that will help both the single and married reader to be the right person for someone else. He offers a fresh perspective for evaluating and improving the reader's love life. 07-5845-5

Other Living Books Best-sellers

THE STORY FROM THE BOOK. From Adam to Armageddon, this book captures the full sweep of the Bible's content in abridged, chronological form. Based on *The Book,* the best-selling, popular edition of *The Living Bible.* 07-6677-6

STRIKE THE ORIGINAL MATCH by Charles Swindoll. Swindoll draws on the best marriage survival guide—the Bible—and his 35 years of marriage to show couples how to survive, flex, grow, forgive, and keep romance alive in their marriage. 07-6445-5

THE STRONG-WILLED CHILD by Dr. James Dobson. Through these practical solutions and humorous anecdotes, parents will learn to discipline an assertive child without breaking his spirit and to overcome feelings of defeat or frustration. 07-5924-9 *Also on Tyndale Living Audio 15-7431-0*

SUCCESS! THE GLENN BLAND METHOD by Glenn Bland. The author shows how to set goals and make plans that really work. His ingredients of success include spiritual, financial, educational, and recreational balances. 07-6689-X

THROUGH GATES OF SPLENDOR by Elisabeth Elliot. This unforgettable story of five men who braved the Auca Indians has become one of the most famous missionary books of all time. 07-7151-6

TRANSFORMED TEMPERAMENTS by Tim LaHaye. An analysis of Abraham, Moses, Peter, and Paul, whose strengths and weaknesses were made effective when transformed by God. 07-7304-7

WHAT WIVES WISH THEIR HUSBANDS KNEW ABOUT WOMEN by Dr. James Dobson. A best-selling author brings us this vital book that speaks to the unique emotional needs and aspirations of today's woman. An immensely practical, interesting guide. 07-7896-0

WHAT'S IN A NAME? Linda Francis, John Hartzel, and Al Palmquist, Editors. This fascinating name dictionary features the literal meaning of hundreds of first names, character qualities implied by the names, and an applicable Scripture verse for each name. 07-7935-5

WHY YOU ACT THE WAY YOU DO by Tim LaHaye. Discover how your temperament affects your work, emotions, spiritual life, and relationships, and learn how to make improvements. 07-8212-7